WIND RIVER ADVENTURES

WIND RIVER ADVENTURES

MY LIFE IN FRONTIER WYOMING

by
EDWARD J. FARLOW

with a foreword by
SHARON KAHIN, PHD.

HIGH PLAINS PRESS

FIRST PRINTING

10 9 8 7 6 5 4 3 2 1

Library of Congress Cataloging-in-Publication Data

Farlow, Edward J., b. 1861.
Wind River adventures : my life in frontier Wyoming /
by Edward J. Farlow with a foreword by Sharon Kahin.
p.   cm.
Includes index.
ISBN 0-931271-46-0.
ISBN 0-931271-45-2 (pbk.)
1. Farlow, Edward J., b. 1861.
2. Pioneers--Wyoming--Wind River Region--Biography.
3. Wind River Region (Wyo.)--Biography.
4. Frontier and pioneer life--Wyoming--Wind River Region.
5. Wind River Indian Reservation (Wyo.)--History.
6. Arapaho Indians--Wyoming--Wind River Region
7. Shoshoni Indians--Wyoming--Wind River Region.
I. Title.
F767.W5F37   1998
978.7'603'092--dc21   98-6951
[b]   CIP

HIGH PLAINS PRESS
539 CASSA ROAD
GLENDO, WYOMING 82213

CONTENTS

FOREWORD

I FIRST BECAME AWARE of the existence of "The Farlow Manuscript" while attending a Western History Conference in Billings, Montana sometime in the late 1980s. "Someone ought to take a look at that and have it published," one of the speakers remarked. I don't remember the speaker's name but his topic was the public "exhibitions" that took place in the late nineteenth and early twentieth centuries that featured Indian dances, arts and crafts and other live demonstrations of Native American culture. Ed Farlow had caught his interest because of the role he played in involving Indians, particularly the Northern Arapaho at Wind River, in movies and show business.

Back home in Dubois, I contacted Tom Bell at the Lander Museum, and we unearthed the *Memoirs* which Farlow had donated to the Lander Pioneer Association. With a grant from the Wyoming Council for the Humanities, the Dubois Museum was able to fund the restoration and duplication of the photographs and pay Loren Jost, now director of the Riverton Museum to research, edit and annotate the text. The project has really been a community effort on the part of all those in Fremont County who are interested in seeing this unique chapter of their past to come to light.

I would like to take this opportunity to thank those who put time and effort into this publication: the Wyoming Council for the Humanities for funding the Dubois Museum's "Wind River

Manuscript Project" as part of their Centennial initiative; Loren Jost for adding excellent footnotes that help guide the uninitiated through this period of history and for tracking down innumerable loose ends, inconsistencies, and somewhat dubious assertions (Farlow was remembered by several who knew him as not only an accomplished storyteller, but also, "something of a wind bag"); Fremont Miller and all the members of the Fremont County Museums Board for agreeing to sponsor the publication; and Nancy Curtis of High Plains Press in Glendo, Wyoming, for her enthusiasm and patience in shepherding this book through to completion.

One final note. While some of the language and expressions in these memoirs, especially as they reflect Farlow's perceptions of, and relationships with, his friends at the Wind River Reservation may sound somewhat condescending to our ears, they should be read and understood within the context of the time they were written. We have chosen to leave Farlow's presentations of the past as he saw and recorded them and trust the reader will understand our reluctance to change or modify word choices that might have served to make his stories and reminiscences more acceptable to modern ears.

SHARON KAHIN, PhD.
DIRECTOR, WIND RIVER HISTORICAL CENTER/
DUBOIS MUSEUM
SEPTEMBER 1998

Early Life

I was born in Dallas County, Iowa in a log cabin in 1861, and lived on a farm on the Coon River when a boy. I was the third boy in the family.

There were eight children in the family, as follows, Henry, Nelson, Edward, Riley, Emma, Elbert (called Zeke), Dolly and Ida. Riley and Emma (now Mrs. Smith) still live in Adel, our old home. Henry died in 1932; Zeke and Ida are living here in Lander; Nelson died in San Francisco in 1929.[1]

Father was a poor man as money goes and I well remember the hungry little bunch that Mother had to feed, and many a good meal I have eaten of mush and milk. We would gather our corn and select the best ears and shell them by hand and Father would take the corn to the grist mill at Adel and bring home three or four sacks of corn meal. I remember how pleased we kids would be when Mother would say we would have plenty to eat for a while, and Mother would make hominy out of the whole corn. We never knew what sugar was and seldom had tea or coffee—only when we had company.

---

[1] Farlow wrote his story in the late 1930s and early 1940s. Henry and Zeke—along with Ed Farlow—all got involved in the stock business in Wyoming. Zeke went on to work as a freighter and later ran an ice business in Lander. He died in 1949. Henry worked on ranches in the Wind River Valley and the Big Horn Basin before settling in Lander. He was elected Fremont County Treasurer in 1907 and Fremont County Clerk in 1911— a position he held for more than 30 years.

As I look back now and see how cheaply we lived, I wonder what our children of today would do if they had to live as we did and yet we had enough and were strong and healthy. We planted a crop of cane and made our own sorghum. We had chickens and cows and pigs. I remember we always had plenty of fat pork and how I hated to eat the fat. I would peel out the lean meat but Father would make me eat the fat as well. Cornmeal and hominy; fruit that Mother had gathered and dried; and I never used a bit of sugar until I left home.

We bought almost nothing and when a package came from the store we were all very anxious to see what it contained. Sometimes it was a new piece of calico for Mother's dress. Ten yards would make a dress then and could be bought for a dollar. Father would haul a load of corn (forty bushels) to town and get four dollars at ten cents a bushel. Once I heard him say "a bushel of corn for a yard of calico."

We had a few sheep and they were shorn and the wool scoured, carded and the spinning wheel would make it into yarn and then Mother's nimble fingers were always going, knitting and weaving for her little flock. And oh, the good warm socks she used to knit. I never wore a stitch of store clothes until I was 14 years old. Then Father got me a suit out of the store and say, wasn't I proud.

But I was not a success as a farmer. My two older brothers, Henry and Nels, as we always called him, were both good hands with the plow and could husk corn like a man. I, being the third son, was turned over to Mother to help her around the house and I became quite handy in the kitchen. But I liked to hunt and trap and go swimming, and that good old Mother of mine would let me go whenever she could spare me. Father would scold her for this and once I heard him say, "Ellen, you are

E. J. Farlow's brother Henry came to Wyoming shortly after his younger brother's arrival in 1876. He spent several years as a cowboy for ranches in the Wind River country and in the Big Horn Basin. Later he served for many years as the Fremont County Treasurer. (Photo courtesy of Pioneer Museum, Lander.)

spoiling that boy by letting him run around so much. He will become worthless and never amount to anything."

When I was 12 years old I was a good shot with the rifle and none of the men in our neighborhood could beat me. Father would never complain when I came in with three or four squirrels which I had knocked from the tops of the tall hickory or oak trees along the river. I heard Father tell a neighbor once that he had three boys all the same size. He said, "Henry is the oldest, Nell is the strongest, and Ed is the grittiest. That little rascal sticks to anything he starts and will go through or bust." I think that remark from Father has helped me many times through life.

When I was 16 years old we had a friend come home to our vicinity who had been working on the Laramie Plains in Wyoming for the last 5 years and he told a glowing account of the west. I found out afterwards that he had exaggerated many things, but it all sounded very good to us then. He was a man about 35 years old and his name was Baxter Anderson. He was working for a man by the name of Tom Alsop who had a ranch on the Big Laramie River, nine miles above the town of Laramie.

First Trip West

So one fine day in April 1876, a chum by the name of William Frakes and I started for Wyoming. We had planned the trip for some two or three weeks. About a week before starting I told Mother we were going to get to Wyoming. She smiled and said, "You will soon be back." But I told her not to say anything to Father, for he would not let me go. Father was boss and made us boys toe the mark.

Leaving the farm about 8 o'clock in the morning, we walked leisurely to Adel, about four miles south. Arriving there about 10 A.M., there were very few people in sight. I remember there was a new set of platform scales in front of Blanchard's Hardware Store and we weighed ourselves on them. Bill weighed 102 pounds. I weighed 98 pounds and I had two suits of clothes. In fact I had on all my clothes (and so did Bill) as I did not dare to start from the house with a bundle of any kind. I had an extra pair of socks in my pocket.

From Adel we went to DeSoto, a small station on the Rock Island Railroad, where we waited for night and a freight train. We had been coached by a fellow who had tramped quite a lot and he had told us how to work it. But it did not work nearly as nice as he told it to us. He said, "Make a station on every train that comes along. They will throw you off at the next station but will not stop between stations to do so." But we did not have the nerve to board a train with the Brakie looking at us.

We were acquainted with a family in DeSoto and we went there and got a good supper. About 9 o'clock a west-bound freight pulled up to the water tank to take water before continuing on west, and we were very sly in getting around the train to keep out of sight of the Brakie. We were told that the brakes were a good place to ride and after the train got started they could not reach us until the train stopped. This was our first experience at beating anything. At least it was mine. Bill had seen a little of it. So we crept slyly under a freight car and mounted the brakes and there we rode the whole night long, and nearly froze as the night got quite cool, but we were making time. Bill was for quitting about midnight but I said "no" as we had no place to go.

The morning found us in Council Bluffs, Iowa. There was one bridge across the Missouri River then and that was the railroad bridge of the Union Pacific. Persons were not allowed to walk across it, as there was a guard at the end. When we approached him to cross he said "no." There were not many trains in those days and we argued with him for some time and tried to get him to let us cross, but he said that it was not allowed.

We drew away; a little strategy was necessary and we decided to try it. Going back to him we engaged him in conversation and asked him several questions as to the way the track was built on the bridge. Bill boldly told him he had worked on a railroad bridge and knew something of them. We were at the end of the bridge examining the spikes when Bill suddenly looked in the direction of Council Bluffs and said, "What is that thing coming down the track?"

The guard looked intently in the direction indicated and we started on a run across the bridge and were making good time. He was after us yelling for us to stop which we had no intention of doing.

"Stop or I will shoot," he shouted.

But we paid no attention and were nearing the west end of the bridge when his yelling attracted the guard at the west end of the bridge. He headed us off and they took us back to the east end of the bridge and threatened to have us locked up. We begged of them to let us go when we were at the west end but to no avail.

We went down to the water's edge and decided we could swim across and carry our clothes on our head as we were both good swimmers. But the water was cold. While we were debating on this a boatman came up to us and asked if we wanted to cross and we said "yes" but we had no money. We really had three dollars and sixty-five cents to start out with and had made up our minds we would not spend a cent unless absolutely necessary. It began to look as if it had become necessary.

After quite a little talk he agreed to row us across for 50 cents and a pocketknife that Bill dug out of his pockets. We made him believe this was all we had.

In Omaha we remembered our advice from the tramp to get out of big towns as they will see you boarding the train and put you off before you start. So we walked toward Papillion, 15 miles west, and slept a good part of the day by the roadside when the sun was warm. Arriving there in the evening we spent 25 cents each at a restaurant for a good meal and I will say that you could get as good a meal then for 25 cents as you can for 75 cents today. This was the first meal for 24 hours as we had made up our minds to live on one meal a day unless more happened to come along.

At 8:30 a freight train pulled in going west and we began to look it over and quite slyly mounted the brakes again just as the train was starting and without being seen. We only rode a station under there as we had a bad seat and it was very dark.

In prowling along the train we discovered a flat car loaded with wagons, buggies and machinery. Into this we crawled and in the center of the load was a large family coach all enclosed and very elaborate. This load was billed to California and by prying around we found we could open one of the doors enough to get inside. T'was a tight squeeze but we made it and in there was a sack of sugar and a fine buffalo robe. To say we were happy is putting it mild. We fairly hugged each other for joy for we knew the Brakie could not get in to us if he tried. We held this berth for twenty-four hours and ate so much sugar as to almost be sick.

Arriving at North Platte the following evening, we decided to get out and get a good square meal and get back in as this was the end of the division and the train would stop there for some time. Out we got as slyly as possible and made straight for a restaurant where we ordered a good meal for 25 cents each, which we ate. The proprietor was a pleasant sort of fellow and asked us which way we were bound and Bill, slapping a half dollar down for the meal, said we were going east.

We made it back to our private car alright and were just climbing on when the Brakie came up and said "You boys have rode far enough, get off."

He said, "Have you got any money?"

We told him no.

"Then you can't ride," he told us.

We then told him that two dollars was all we had and he said, "T'aint enough, I will let you ride 50 miles for that." We did not think that was enough and told him so and he watched us so close that we were unable to get out of town on that train.

We went up town then and bummed around the saloons for two or three hours as these were new to us, neither of us ever having been in a saloon before. About midnight we saw a nasty fight between a white man and a Mexican in which a knife was used and the white man was badly cut up.

After this we hunted around the edge of the town and found a haystack into which we burrowed and spent the rest of the night.

North Platte was not much of a town at that time. As I remember, it was about one block on Main Street, perhaps 300 or 400 people.

We went back to the restaurant where we had our supper the night before. We needed breakfast as we were both hungry as bears and the motion to eat was unanimously carried. The proprietor recognized us as the boys of the evening before and asked us if we were railroading, to which Bill replied "you bet," which was quite a smart saying for those days.

The front on the restaurant was a little cigar store and the dining room was through a small door and the kitchen was behind. A Chinaman was doing the cooking. When we had finished our breakfast Bill discovered the Chinaman going across the street from the back of the restaurant. A thought came to him and he said, "You go out through the front and tell the proprietor if he asks you that I will pay the bill when I come out." This I did. No sooner had I left the table than Bill went out the back door.

We were to get out of town to the west on the railroad track as soon as possible and I do not know how long the restaurant man waited before he looked for Bill. But I did not lie to him as Bill told me he would pay him as soon as he came out the front way and he was not yet come out that way.

Before going to breakfast that morning we had a little council talk in regard to Bill's pants. He was almost in rags and needed a pair of overalls very bad, so we decided to invest. We got him a pair for ninety cents so when we suddenly left town Bill

had on a new pair of pants. We walked to the first station west
of North Platte, sleeping a good part of the day as that was the
only rest we got.

Arriving at Offallon station we found an Irish woman there
at the section house and she was very talkative and a fine woman. We told her we were trying to get to Laramie and had work
there which was a guess on our part for no one there knew we
were even coming. We asked her how about a little something
to eat as we were broke.

She said "I will be only too glad to feed you and help you on
your way. You seem to be good boys and have been well raised."

After setting us a very good meal we left with a "God bless
you both" from that noble woman.

We waited at the water tank for a freight which arrived in due
time and we boarded the brakes again. But it was very cold this
night and we froze out about two o'clock. So we quit the train
east of Ogallala which we made the next day and spent our last
cent for something to eat. That night we boarded a freight but decided it was too cold for the brakes and decided to ride the
bumpers. But we were discovered by the brakeman as we were
getting on and soon he came over the train looking between the
cars for us. He flashed his lantern down on us standing there
between the two cars and said "What the hell you doing there?"

We replied, "Riding."

"Got any money?" was the first thing he said.

We replied, "No."

"Then you will have to get off now."

To this we made no answer.

"Get off or I will knock you off," he said.

"Come ahead," we replied.

At this he started for the back end of the train saying he
would get us out of there. After he had gone, we climbed upon

the top of the train and soon we saw the light of his lantern come upon the train from the caboose. He came toward us and we retreated to the very front of the train, keeping about a car length ahead of him.

We climbed down to the coal tender and we went up to the engine and the engineer asked us, "What the hell are you boys doing here?"

We told him we were trying to get away from the Brakie who was then standing on the end of the car overlooking the tender. He called to the engineer to "put them little sons of bitches off at the first stop." The engineer's reply was that he would attend to us.

After the Brakie was gone the engineer asked us a few questions and seeing we were half froze told us to grab a shovel and shovel coal into the engine which we did and rode into Cheyenne with them. The fireman enjoyed the trip as much as we did, and this engineer was one of nature's noblemen. I did not get his name as I did not know at this time that this kind of man was so scarce.

When we arrived in Cheyenne and the train was stopped he said, "Boys, you wait for me on the corner over there and when I get my engine put away we will go and get something to eat."

We waited and soon he came and took us up town and gave us a good meal and paid for it and bid us good-bye and good luck. We left Cheyenne with a very light heart and walked to Sherman which is on the continental divide and the highest point on the U.P. Road. Sleeping a good part of the day here we awaited for a train. The nights were very cold and we could not stand it to ride far. We had to quit the train and gather a lot of old ties and build a fire and in this we were joined by two other hobos. After the sun was up we started for Laramie, our destination.

ALSOP'S RANCH ON THE LARAMIE PLAINS

WALKING FAST WE arrived there about 10 o'clock in the morning and soon found a little restaurant where they knew both Baxter Anderson and Alsop.[1] Here we searched ourselves for the price of something to eat and I found in the pocket of my vest six three-cent stamps and my pocketknife which went for a little handout at the restaurant.

The man showed us the road out of town toward the Alsop ranch, saying, "You can't miss it as it is the old stage station of the Overland Stage Company and is straight up the river nine miles."

---

[1] Tom Alsop is closely associated with the beginnings of Wyoming's stock industry. Many readers are familiar with the story about a freighter being caught in a snowstorm on Sherman Hill in 1863. The freighter was making a return run from Salt Lake City to Omaha and when weather conditions deteriorated he turned his teams of oxen loose and then rode with his men quickly toward Omaha in an effort to save their own lives. The oxen were expected to die. But when the freighter returned the next spring to salvage what he could of the wagons, he found the oxen alive and fat, grazing at the southern end of the Laramie Plains. The incident is, supposedly, what sparked the idea that Wyoming might provide good cattle range. The freighter who made the discovery was Tom Alsop.

Alsop was employed by Omaha's commercial tycoon Ed Creighton at the time and that association continued for a number of years. But in 1869, after Creighton's contract to help with the grading of the Union Pacific railway was complete, Alsop established his ranch at the stage crossing on the Big Laramie River, south of the current town of Laramie. Seven years later, Ed Farlow arrived at that ranch.

So we started and about noon, tired out and sleepy, we both went to sleep and must have slept by the roadside for about five hours. We were then about three miles from the ranch and I was never so completely turned around in my life before or since as I was when I woke up. The country had reversed itself and it seemed to me we must go toward Laramie to reach the ranch. Bill and I had quite an argument about it. Bill was undecided but I was sure and we were about to start out in the opposite direction when a man came along on horseback. We asked him where Alsop's ranch was and he said about three miles right up the road and that decided us.

So we lit out and arrived at the ranch just in time for supper. Neither Anderson or Alsop were there but they asked us in and we ate. They showed us the bunkhouse and Anderson's bed and we went to bed at sundown and they had to call us in the morning for breakfast. That was the first bed we had slept in since leaving home, just seven days ago.

They told us that Anderson and Alsop were over on the Little Laramie where Alsop had another ranch. He was fencing and improving and they did not know if he wanted any more help or not.

After breakfast we decided to go over there as it was only 15 miles and we were feeling fine after the good supper and breakfast and about 12 hours good sleep. The trip across the plains that beautiful day was one of the most enjoyable days of my life. We were young and strong and full of life and had not a care on earth and this was all new to us. The plains were covered with antelope, some of which we got very close to. We saw a coyote and some eagles and lots of prairie dogs and it was well toward evening when we arrived at the Little Laramie ranch where we found both Anderson and Alsop.

Anderson asked Alsop if he could use either of us, remarking at the time that "that boy of Farlow's is a damn good worker." So

I was engaged to go to work the next morning. As Alsop was going back to the home ranch that day he said he would take Bill with him as he thought his neighbor Hutton,[2] who lived just across the river, might use him.

Alsop appeared to me as if he did not think much of my ability as a worker, as Bill was the huskier of us two. I think if he had not been influenced by Anderson's talk he would have kept Bill. However, he told me to get some gunny sacks and get up on an old shed and pull the wool off a lot of dead sheep. The sheep had drifted under the shed during the winter and had died. The snow had just melted off them enough that they had been thrown upon the shed to ripen up, as Tom called it. Someone had pulled the wool off a part of them but the most of them were untouched and they were sure ripe enough. They were rotten and there was about a dozen that had been partly pulled.

Tom and Bill left and Anderson saddled up his horse and rode off so I was left alone with my job. I climbed up on the shed and started in. After pulling wool for about 10 minutes I got very sick, as the stench was terrible. I vomited up my breakfast. After resting for a few minutes I started in again but soon had to quit. For about an hour I was the sickest boy you ever saw. I would go and get a drink of water and bathe my head and go back and throw it up. I had about decided to quit the job when I recalled my father's words, "Ed is the grittiest, and when he starts in on anything he will go through or bust." But in this case it looked very much like a bust.

However, after finding out that a drink of water was the worst thing for me, I rested awhile and went at it again. My

---

[2] Charley Hutton and Tom Alsop had been friends while working for Ed Creighton. They established ranches on the Laramie Plains at the same time. Alsop's ranch was on the west side of the Big Laramie stage crossing. Hutton's ranch was on the east side.

stomach was empty and I could throw up no more. After a little I got so I could stand the stench and I tore into those sheep and got rid of about half of them by noon. Anderson did not show up at noon and I got a bite to eat and rested and felt pretty good. At about 1:30 I started in again and it was as in the morning. In 10 minutes I had got rid of my dinner and was very sick and I thought sure it was all over. However I rested and would go back and try again and after about an hour I was able to stand it and again tore into those sheep and finished the job about 5:30.

I had got myself pretty well washed up when Anderson arrived, but my clothes smelled horrible. Anderson smiled but said nothing and after supper he put on a boiler of water and warmed it. He had me strip and I put on a shirt and pants of his and took off all my clothes. He had me washing clothes until bedtime as I had to have them to dry for the morrow. Anderson was a tall man and I looked worse than Charley Chaplin in his clothes. I could see Anderson laughing to himself as he would look at me but it was all right with me and I was earning money for Alsop told me if I was any good he would pay me $35 a month. When I left Iowa they were hiring the best farm hands for $17 a month and it seemed almost unbelievable to me that I, a mere boy, would be paid such an enormous price. If Alsop had paid me off at $10 a month, I would have been satisfied.

The next evening Alsop returned with some seed grain and he was going to sow. When he drove up, Anderson told me to step lively and unhitch the team. I was a good hand with a team and promptly did as I was told.

About the first thing Anderson said to Alsop was, "Well, Tom, the kid has got all the wool off the sheep."

Tom gave a loud Ha Ha and said, "Good for him."

Turning, he said, "That is the third man I have put at that job."

He then asked me if I could plow and I told him yes. He had a new 14-inch plow and a good big span of mules. He told me the next morning to hitch the mules to the plow and plow up a piece of ground that had been plowed the year before and planted to something, as he intended to try some oats in it this year. This is the only lot of ground that I remember seeing plowed on the Laramie Plains that year. However there might have been others as I was gone a good part of the summer. This lot of ground was long and in good condition for plowing and contained about five acres.

Alsop left the next morning as he was going most of the time looking after his two ranches and his horses and cattle that were running on the open range. I hooked the mules on the walking plow and was at home behind it. For a time I thought I was on the old farm on the Coon River in Iowa. The mules were good walkers and at noon I had quite a lot plowed.

I asked Anderson how much the mules could stand, as I was not used to mules. He said, "If you can play those damn mules out, I would like to see you do it. Don't slow down on their account."

It was the boast of most of the Iowa boys at that time that they could play out almost any team walking behind a good plow, for a plow that is running right is a big help to the man walking behind it as he has the handles to hold to which is a great help in a day's walking.

In two days I finished the piece and the next day, slinging a sack over my shoulders, I sowed it. Then, hitching to the harrow, I dragged it over twice before night, just in time to get my team put away as Alsop drove up. That night it came up quite a storm and Alsop was very well pleased that I had done so well. He took me over to the home ranch, gave me a good saddle horse and a soft job herding about fifty brood mares.[3]

About this time there arrived at the ranch a couple of trappers and miners by the name of George Garoutte and Mike. They called him Red Mike, and I do not remember his last name. He was the older and more experienced of the two.

They were old friends of Alsop and I believe he went in with them on what they might find and grubstaked them, as they say.

Alsop said to Mike, "Why don't you take the kid along? I don't need him here for the present." They were expecting to be gone into the mountains on a prospecting trip for a couple of months.

They talked it over for a short time and Mike turned to me and said, "Kid, do you want to go along?"

Did I want to go along? Say, I would have given the shirt off my back to go. I had read a few dime novels in Iowa about digging gold and killing Indians, and here was the chance right before me. I thought as much as could be that I would go out in the mountains and get a few bags of gold and a few scalps and go back to Iowa rich and famous.

---

[3] Alsop sold his ranch on the Big Laramie and moved to the Little Laramie in 1880. He was known for the fine shorthorn cattle he raised and a type of light horse which was well suited for pulling streetcars in the cities. He died in 1889 while driving into Laramie on stock business

Alsop's brand—TA—deserves special mention. Alsop sold the brand and a bunch of cattle to a doctor who moved the cattle and the brand to his ranch in Johnson County. It was at that ranch where a small army of gunmen hired by members of the Wyoming Stock Growers' Association tried to eliminate homesteaders and settlers whom the association considered to be rustlers.

PROSPECTING

S o I WENT along.
They said I would not have much to do. They gave me a good Henry rifle and lots of ammunition. I think each of us had 200 rounds and a good horse and saddle. And we had four pack horses and an extra saddle horse; in all eight head of horses. All I had to do was to jump up in the morning and start the fire and go get the horses and saddle them up and wash the dishes and peel the potatoes and put on the coffee and unsaddle and hobble the horses and bring the wood and water. They would sit and smoke their pipes and talk about formations and anticlines and washes and bedrock. I would be tired as a dog at night.

When they were sinking to bedrock for a test of panning I would jump in and dig like a beaver as I expected at any time to be rolling in gold. My ardor began to cool after two or three weeks and we had found nothing.

We went northwest from Laramie and crossed the Platte somewhere near where Casper now stands. I never did know just where we did go as I was not interested as to where we went. This was a new country to Garoutte but Mike had been through here before and knew the country.

The Indians were bad at this time and we advanced very cautiously, following—for the most part—in the draws. We saw a band of Indians on the head of Dry Powder River in the distance. They were evidently a war party as we did not see any sign of squaws, lodge poles or tepees. We kept well out of sight and that night we ate our supper without making a fire. For a few days we advanced very carefully whenever we were coming out into the open or crossing a divide. One or both of the men would dismount and advance very carefully and peer on ahead frequently. They would lie down and crawl to the top of a ridge to scan the country before exposing our outfit to the danger of being discovered. This Mike seemed to be a very shrewd plainsman.

One evening when we had traveled for most of the day without prospecting, we came near to the top of a ridge and stopping, Mike said, "We will see the Big Horn River from the top and there may be some Indians camped on it." So they dismounted and crawled to the summit and laid there for so long I got impatient holding the horses. Tying them to some scrub cedar near me, I crawled up beside them to see what it was that was keeping them. Not more than a quarter of a mile away there were two Indian tepees and Mike was just saying, "That is Scorrell's outfit. I know that pinto horse because I trapped with him two years ago on the head of Green River and he said he was going to move over on the Big Horn this year."

They had seen but one man and a woman and two children while watching there for nearly an hour.

The bunch of horses could be plainly seen and a bay and white spotted one (the pinto) were plainly to be seen among the bunch. Mike said, "We will take a chance anyhow, and if it is Scorrell we are lucky for he knows these hills like a book."

Now I had been taught on this trip and it had been pounded into my head never to go any place without my gun. Mike said, "Take it with you to bed, take it when you go for a pail of water or a stick of wood. In fact, never leave it out of your hand

and if you see anything suspicious get down at once and stay down until you know what it is." I had practiced this until I was good at it and they would try and catch me without my gun and once Mike did. I went but a short distance from the camp to get some wood and he popped up from behind a log and said, "Now I have you." After that I could drop to the ground as quick as a flash at the approach of danger.

We took our outfit and went down to the river and sure enough it was Scorrell. He was a Canadian half-breed, French and Indian, and was married to a Sioux squaw. They had two children, which I later came to know very well. Annie, a girl of twelve, and Norceese, a boy of ten. I later found this same family camped near Lander where they lived for several years.

The trappers were glad to see each other and as our men had a couple of jugs of good whiskey, as they called it, they enjoyed the evening together. I did not drink whiskey then nor ever afterwards. I saw so much trouble and misery and ill feeling caused from it that I decided to let it alone and I have never cared for a drink that most men seem so crazy about.

Scorrell told them what he thought of the prospects around there and said he would like to have them help him build a corral to catch his horses in as he had only been in there about a week. They said, "We will leave the kid with you. He is a good worker and we will leave part of our outfit here and look these hills over for a few days."

This they did and I started in the next morning to build a round corral as he wanted. I enjoyed dragging the poles from quite a distance with a saddle horse and rope from the horn of the saddle. I think it was the end of the third day that I had the corral all finished. I had soaked a buffalo hide in the river to soften it so as to cut it in strips to tie the posts and poles in place. I was just finishing the bars when I looked down the river to the northeast about a half a mile and saw two Indians coming. True to my training, I dropped to the ground and, with my gun in my hand, lay behind a fence post to see what would happen. I had been taught that an Indian will kill a white man whenever he gets a chance and it is up to the white man to beat him to it. At least that was Mike's and George's theory.

MY FIRST INDIANS

THE INDIANS RODE directly to the lodges as if they knew where they were going and got off and went inside. They stayed in there for nearly an hour and all the time I laid there. I was getting quite impatient and was about to take to the brush but thought they might be watching me from inside the tepees. They came out at last and mounted their horses and rode on up the river. After they had gone, I went to the tepee and Scorrell said they were a couple of Arapahos and they had been in a hell of a big fight with the white soldiers and Sioux on the Greasy Grass (meaning the Little Big Horn River). They said the Indians had killed all the soldiers and were coming up this way.

When he said that I guess he saw alarm written on my face for he at once said, "They will not harm us, as the old woman will see them first and we will be all right." But I was very doubtful about this and for the first time wished I was back on the farm. I did not want scalps half as bad as I thought I did. As for gold, I had not found any so far.

The next day Mike and George came back. When they were told what the Indians said about the big fight Mike said it was General Crook and remarked, "He got it last."[1]

---

[1] It's difficult to determine exactly what the author means here. General George Crook was not involved in the Custer battle, although he was camped with a large force of men on the east side of the Big Horn Mountains. Mike may have known that General Crook was in the area and could have surmised that it was Crook's men who were killed.

But this was the Custer fight and those were two young Arapahos who had left the Shoshone reservation and joined the Sioux in their camp on the Greasy Grass and had been in the fight. Knowing the troops would go after the Indians stronger than ever, they were slipping back to their reservation and no one would know they had been in the fight.[2]

It is a strange thing that the Indians at Camp Brown on the Little Wind River knew of the fight and the result before the commanding officer of that post received the news by wire.[3]

---

[2] The Arapaho Indians were not placed on the Shoshone Indian Reservation until March of 1878—almost two years after Custer and his men lost their lives on the Little Bighorn. However, there are frequent reports of Arapaho camps in the area surrounding the reservation throughout the late 1860s and '70s and these men may have been returning to one of those camps.

The involvement of several Arapahos in the Custer fight is mentioned in several sources. In his autobiography, cowboy movie star Tim McCoy recalls a 1919 conversation at Ethete in which Left Hand and Water Man acknowledged their participation in the event. They identified themselves as being a part of group of five Arapahos who were in the Indian camp on the Little Bighorn on June 25, 1876. The others were Yellow Eagle, Yellow Fly, and a Southern Arapaho named Well-Knowing (sometimes known as Green Grass). On page 131 of this manuscript, Ed Farlow says there were 25 Arapahos in the Indian camp on the Little Big Horn.

Left Hand said the Arapahos slipped away from the main camp of Sioux and Cheyenne on the second night after the battle. He and Water Man rode hard to Fort Robinson (in northwestern Nebraska) where they had been employed as scouts by the Army. Military records confirm the employment of Left Hand and Water Man as scouts at Fort Robinson in 1876. But Yellow Eagle, Yellow Fly, and Green Grass are not listed. Perhaps two of them were the Indians who rode into Scorrell's camp on the Big Horn River.

[3] Camp Brown was established as Camp Augur in June of 1869 on the site which is now Fifth and Main streets in Lander. The name was changed to Camp Brown in March of 1870. The post was dismantled and moved to the present site of Fort Washakie in 1871

These were the Shoshone and Arapaho Indians and at peace with the white men.

Mike and George did not seem to be worried much about the news and said "We will get out of here." The next morning we packed up and disappeared in the hills. We prospected the head of No Wood, a tributary of the Big Horn, the Sweetwater Mountains south of Split Rock and Devil's Gate and found some very good colors, but nothing big. The last of July found us back on the Laramie Plains.

Nothing but routine life on the ranch until the spring of 1879. In the latter part of May, Bronco Sam[4] and I took a bunch of 50 horses to Senator Warren's ranch on Pole Creek not far from Cheyenne. This was the first time I met F.E. Warren, who was not a Senator then. He took a fancy to me and asked me to go to work for him but I said I had a job with Alsop on the TA Ranch and had no reason to quit him.[5]

No sooner were we back to Alsop's ranch when he sold 100 horses to a rancher in Nebraska about 100 miles east of North Platte. Baxter Anderson, Sam and I were sent to deliver them. Bronco Sam was a Spaniard and was a champion rider at that time and was employed breaking broncos for Alsop.

---

[4] Bronco Sam was of Spanish and African descent. His real name was Sam Stewart, though few knew him by that name. Most knew him as one of the best bronc busters in Wyoming and for his ability to gentle "hot-blooded" horses. When Sam caught his wife with another man, he shot both of them and then turned the gun on himself. He died nine days later.

[5] Francis E. Warren was an early, major stockman in the area around Cheyenne. He served as a legislator in Wyoming's territorial days and also as Wyoming's territorial governor in 1885–86 and 1889–1890. He led the effort to attain statehood for Wyoming and served briefly as the State of Wyoming's first governor before being appointed to the U.S. Senate. When he died in 1929 he had served more than 37 years in the Senate and it would be more than three decades before anyone would surpass that record.

We took a pack outfit and started with the 100 head of mixed range horses and were 17 days on the trail. We had to night herd for a week, after which time Anderson or Sam would stay with them until eleven o'clock and then go to bed. We would be after them at daylight. We had no trouble and delivered the horses at the ranch.

Anderson's instructions were to sell the saddle and pack horses and return on the train. We stayed there a week trying to sell the horses but could not find a buyer. I rode east as far as Grand Island to see a man whom we heard might buy them but he would not even come to look at them.

When I returned and told Anderson, he said, "I will not give them to these damn grangers. Sam, you and the boy bring the outfit home, I'm going on the next train."

So Sam and I trailed the outfit home to the Big Laramie and in this way I learned the Overland Trail almost from Omaha to the South Pass in Wyoming.[6]

Shortly after returning to the TA Ranch I got a letter from George Garoutte from Miner's Delight, Wyoming wanting us to come there. So Bill Frakes and I again rode the rods from Laramie to Green River; we went through to Miner's Delight on the stage. Bill died a few years later at Pacific Springs, Wyoming.

When we arrived at Miner's Delight we found that Garoutte and a partner, having not heard from me, had started on their trip. You might as well hunt for a needle in a haystack as a

---

[6] What we know today as the Overland Trail does not go through South Pass. The Oregon-California Trail went through South Pass and it was that trail that was used by emigrants and the first overland stage company. In 1862, the Overland stage and mail route was moved south because of Indian attacks on stations along the Oregon-California Trail route. That southern route is the route that is generally referred to as the Overland Trail. There are, however, frequent examples of Wyoming pioneers referring to both routes as the Overland Trail

prospector in the mountains, so I got a job with a man by the name of Louis Miller who was just moving down on Beaver Creek, near Warm Spring,[7] 12 miles below Miner's Delight. Miller was going to start a small dairy to supply the mines with milk and butter and I helped to build the first permanent cabin on Beaver.

---

[7]This is the location that later became known as Hailey. Hailey was best known as the stage station at the bottom of the notorious Beaver Hill on the old Rawlins-Lander road. People who live in the area say the warm spring stopped flowing after an oil well was drilled nearby.

THE LANDER VALLEY

B ILL WENT ON DOWN to the Lander Valley and I did not see him until the next June. I worked for Miller fifteen months and during that time I rode the range quite a lot looking after his cattle as Miller was near-sighted and was not a good range hand. I helped to put in several issues of beef at the Shoshone Agency during this time and this was my first meeting with the Indians.

An incident occurred in the summer of 1879 that I will never forget. There was an uprising of the Ute Indians in Colorado. They went on the warpath, killing their agent (Nathan Meeker) and the 26 employees, left the reservation and started out killing and plundering.[1] The news came to the mines.

I will say here that the mines consisted of the South Pass mining district that was discovered in 1868. There had been a

---

[1] Trouble brewed on the Ute Reservation throughout the summer of 1879. But it wasn't until the fall that events finally reached a violent climax. Indian Agent Nathan Meeker had angered the Utes with his insistence that they engage in agricultural pursuits and by plowing meadows which had been used as pasture for horses. In mid-September, with the possibility of trouble on the reservation increasing, Major T.T. Thornburgh marched with 140 men and 33 supply wagons toward the Ute reservation from Fort Steele, near Rawlins. When the Utes learned of the advancing military unit they became alarmed. Representatives of the tribes met with Meeker at the agency and with Major Thornburgh as he advanced. They asked Thornburgh to halt his move and to travel to the agency for a meeting with tribal

big rush in there at that time and a large amount of gold was taken out, but the mines were failing even at this time. There had sprung up three towns about three miles apart; South Pass, Atlantic City and Miner's Delight. Even at this date the miners were leaving by the hundreds and hunting for better diggings, as they called it.

A rider was sent out to alarm the settlers that the Indians were out and to come in to the settlements. We had received this word but we were doing so well and were in an out-of-the-way place. There were two trappers and hunters camped just below us who thought we would not be found and so we stayed there. Mrs. Miller was always watching for Indians. I had at that time an Army carbine, a very good gun, and we always had plenty of ammunition on hand.

During the winter of 1878 and '79 we were short of food for about twenty hogs that we had been feeding on skim milk and slops. When the cows went dry in the late fall we had to rustle for feed. Miller got some corn at Camp Brown once but not much and so he told me to kill elk, deer and antelopes and feed the meat to the hogs which I did. In the spring it looked like a bone yard around the ranch. There were thousands of wild game in the country at that time and many a morning I got up and looking out would see an elk, deer or antelope within range of

---

chiefs and Agent Meeker. Fearing a trap, Thornburgh refused. When Thornburg's command crossed the Milk River—the northern boundary of the Ute Reservation—they were met by a force of armed Indians. Shooting began and in the fight that followed Thornburgh was shot and killed. Ten other soldiers and 23 Utes also died in the fighting.

With the die cast, the Utes descended on the White River Agency on September 29 and killed Meeker and nine of his employees. They took Meeker's wife and daughter along with another woman and her two children as captives.

my gun and would knock it down and skin it for the hogs, cutting out a few choice parts for ourselves. We gathered up and burned the bones of about seventy-five of these splendid wild animals that I had killed that winter. I think now of the terrible waste we all practiced at that time. Many a fine deer and antelope have I shot and just took the saddle as we called it (short hind quarters) and I left the rest of the animal lying on the plains.

One morning about 10 o'clock, as I was under the bank of the creek working near the house, Mrs. Miller came running and said, "I see Indians." We went into the house and closed the door. I told her if we would keep still perhaps they would think there was no one at home and go away. We had a heavy hewn log cabin built for defense and a heavy dirt roof and a very heavy door. But we had not cut port holes in the cabin. The Indians were all on reservations, had signed the peace treaty, and Miller thought there was no danger. For the fastening of the door we had a heavy bar to drop in place and a heavy brace to reach to the opposite side of the building. For every day use we had just a button to hold the door shut.

We closed the door and buttoned it and put the bar in place. But the bar did not touch the door by about two inches. I peeked out of the one small window and saw the Indians coming and counted them. There were fifteen. I laid out 20 cartridges on the table and thought that would be enough to kill all of them. I was a dead shot and did not expect to waste any ammunition on them.

I remember I was not much scared as they came around the house. Mrs. Miller had two curtains over the window and they could not see in. She began to moan and wring her hands and I sternly told her to keep still. One Indian tried the door. They evidently knew we were in there as he kept trying to open the door and saying in English, "Ope Door."

I was getting a little more nervous all the time and soon I heard them grinding their knives on our grindstone and my hair began to stand straight up and I became thoroughly frightened. I had my gun in hand, cocked and ready to start shooting. The Indian at the door at this time pushed so hard on it that the button gave away and the door dropped in against the bar leaving a space of about an inch to which the Indian applied his eye to look in. He looked square into the muzzle of my gun about two feet away. He just dodged back in time to save his life as I was just pulling the trigger when he disappeared. There was much jabbering among them then and I heard them moving away and then all was still.

I was sure I could smell smoke and at once I thought they had set the house afire and were waiting for us to come out. This suspense was terrible and Mrs. Miller was about to collapse.

I said, "Take a peek."

She peeked while I stood with my gun ready and said, "I see soldiers."

Now if that was not the most welcome message a boy ever received then I am no judge.

I stepped to the window and drawing up the corner of the blind looked up the draw in the same direction the Indians had come. There, about a quarter of a mile away, came the soldiers. At their head rode two men, one of them bearing the stars and stripes. Do you blame me for loving the stars and stripes? It was the most welcome sight a man or a boy and a lone woman ever saw and I shed tears as I write this today at the thought of that time. I can never, even to this day, tell of this event without breaking down.

The Indians had seen the troops coming before we did and fled. The Army captain later said he saw them leaving. Soon the soldiers rode up to the cabin door and gave a knock.

A man said, "Hello, anybody home?"

I opened the door and when he saw me he said, "Hello, boy, were you scared?"

I told him no, but I guess he could see that I was about half scared to death as he smiled.

Then, discovering the woman, who had fainted dead away, he exclaimed, "My God, are you here alone with this woman?"

I told him Miller and the two trappers had gone to Miner's Delight and should be back at any time.

He asked, "Did you get any word to come in, as the Indians were out?"

"Yes," I replied, "but the men thought it was not necessary."

This was almost a miracle as these troops had come from Fort Washakie that morning forty miles to answer a call for help coming from Major Thornburg's command which had gone in pursuit of the Utes who had left the reservation after killing the agent and all the employees. The Utes had turned and ambushed Thornburg's troops and surrounded them and the Major and a number of troops had been killed.[2] But he got word out by a scout who had ridden to Fort Steele. They wired to Fort Washakie and Fort Russell for help. These troops received the message at 3 o'clock that morning and at 5 o'clock were on their way and had made forty miles already.[3] The scout and guide Frank Grouard knew of the trail through Red Canyon on the Beaver, a short cut, and brought the troops that way. That was the only thing that saved us.

---

[2] As noted earlier, the Ute Indians battled Thornburg's force on the Milk River before killing Meeker and nine employees at the agency.

[3] Couriers from Thornburg's force reached Rawlins with the news during the early morning hours of October 1.

The troops camped there for about two hours, fed and rested their horses, drank up all the good milk and cream we had, and went on their way. Miller and the two trappers came back before the troops went.

These troops made Fort Steele the next day and were met there by troops from Fort Russell and made a forced march to where Thornburg's command was being held by the Indians and relieved them. Without this splendid movement by these troops, Thornburg's command would have suffered the fate of Custer's command.[4]

---

[4] By the morning of October 2, Colonel Wesley Merritt and troops from Fort Russell (Cheyenne) were in Rawlins and ready to head south. Authoritative sources make no mention of involvement by troops from Fort Washakie. It is possible that a small force of troops from Fort Washakie under a junior officer might have been consolidated with Merritt's troops. Additional research is needed on the role of Fort Washakie troops.

Merritt arrived on Milk Creek on the morning of October 5. The Utes had held Thornburg's command under siege until Merritt's arrival. Additional troops were being rushed to the scene as well, including units from as far away as Texas. Although Army generals urged quick and forceful punishment of the Utes, Interior Secretary Carl Schurz' emissary negotiated a peaceful resolution and the safe release of the women and children captives.

BACK TO IOWA

THE UTES FINALLY surrendered and went back on their reservation but they were always a lot of trouble and McLaughlin describes them as the "unwhipped Utes."[1]

That fall, about the first of November, peace having been restored and no Indians being known to be at large, I decided to go home to see the old folks in Iowa. Taking a bundle on my back I walked from Miller's ranch on Beaver to Rawlins, about 100 miles. There was no road from Rawlins to Lander at this time as all the freight, mail and express came in from Green River City on the Union Pacific through the mines and Lander to Fort Washakie. Lander was then only a stage station on the mail and freight road.

I had a horse but did not know what I would do with it if I rode to Rawlins, which was closer than Green River and 125 miles east. I knew of a cabin in Crooks Gap where a couple of men were staying and I knew the country, for by this time I was getting to be quite an experienced mountaineer, although but 18 years old. I took it easy and got to Rawlins in three-and-one-half days. I was pretty footsore as I had not done much walking and being a cowboy I had on a pair of high-heeled boots which are poor for walking.

---

[1] James McLaughlin was for many years the government's leading negotiator in its dealings with Indian tribes. In 1904 he negotiated the agreement with the Shoshone and Arapaho Indians which led to the opening of a large portion of the Wind River Reservation for settlement by non-Indians.

I spent the winter at home on the farm in Dallas County with the folks and went to school.

In the spring Father said, "Well, Ed, are you going to stay with us? I will give you wages if you will and we would like to have you."

I said, "How much wages?"

He answered, "Fifteen dollars per month."

This was the going wages at that time and I told him I had a job waiting for me at $49 a month.

So my brother Nelson, two years older than I, rigged up a team and wagon and on the 21st day of April, 1880 we started from Adel, Iowa in a covered wagon to drive to Wyoming.

We were six days to Omaha, having ferried over the Missouri that evening. In Omaha we found 41 teams all ready to cross the plains. The next day being Sunday, and there being a jolly crowd in camp, we rested. That night they had a big medicine talk and we were going to start the next morning. Some of the teams had been there for a week waiting for company, afraid to start.

They organized that night and elected a captain and made all the arrangements as to distance of travel, places in the train and so on. They were all done but hiring a guide. There was a man there—a short Buffalo Bill-looking fellow—that wanted the job and had been trying for two or three days to land it. But nothing definite had been done. I remember that night he made quite a speech. He had a very long gun and a fierce looking knife at his belt. I did not like the looks of the fellow. He was western alright and had evidently got down to Omaha and was broke and looking for a chance to get back. If he had not been so unreasonable they might have hired him. He told them how bad the Indians were and the dangers of getting on the wrong trail.

But you could not get off the Overland Trail anymore than you could leave the Union Pacific Railroad, it was that plain. A great highway 100 feet wide in most places.

He told them of the dangers from robbers and highwaymen and outlaws and made up quite a story. He asked them for five dollars a day, a saddle horse to be furnished him, and board.

They were all ready to vote on the proposition when my brother turned to me and said, "What are we going to do?" He had got acquainted with a bunch from Missouri that day and there were five good mule teams and two of the boys were about the size and age of my brother. He had told them of my experience on the plains.

Up to this time I said nothing and in reply to Nel's question I said, "We will hitch up early in the morning and pull out. I know the trail better than that fellow does and we want to make 25 miles a day at least as we have a good job waiting for us there."

One of the big Missourians got up and said, "This boy has been across the plains four times and knows every foot of the way and says he is going to hitch up and pull out in the morning and expects to make 25 miles a day and if his team can do that so can my mules and we are going to follow him."

That ended the council and for six days I led that train. Some dropped out and we overtook some others so that when we reached the ranch where I had helped deliver the horses in 1878 we still had 42 wagons. We camped near the ranch and the owner came to our camp and recognized me and gave us some good advice as he was a real plainsman.

He said, "You will have no trouble with Indians, but look out for horse thieves. There are two bands of them working on the trail between here and Cheyenne." He named them and said one bunch were holding out at Plum Creek, a short distance west, and advised us to corral our stock from now on, which we did.

That is where I learned to corral wagons either in stockade formation or battle formation as the occasion might require. This knowledge came in very handy in the making of that great picture *The Covered Wagon*, in which I was called upon to handle the Indians.

We traveled a little slower from there, still driving the lead wagon. The captain of the train was called Uncle Billy. He was a fine old man with long gray whiskers and he had a married son and son-in-law. In all they had four wagons. He was very nice to me and, as I have thought afterwards, for a very good purpose. He would ask me how far it was to the next water and also as to feed. I would tell him freely all I knew about it as it had been only two years since I had trailed over it and everything was very clear to me.

Along towards evening he would say, "My boy, pick us out a nice camp." I was very proud of being able to guide this train and would ride ahead as I had a very good horse and would select the camp and guide the wagons into position and became an expert in corralling wagons.

Before we got to Cheyenne, at Sidney, some of the wagons took another road and went into Colorado. And at Cheyenne some of them went south and from there on west. We did not corral as I was well acquainted with the country and the people and did not think it necessary. At Rawlins we quit the train and went north to Miller's ranch and to Lander where we located.

IN THE STOCK BUSINESS

I WENT TO WORK FOR a cattleman named R.H. Hall who used the Square and Compass brand.[1] There were lots of cattle coming into Wyoming at that time and they were stocking the range very rapidly from Oregon, Washington and Utah from the west, and from Texas in the south.

I worked for the Square and Compass outfit until the fall of 1881. In the fall of 1880 I bought 100 head of yearling heifers from W.P. Noble.[2] My brothers, Henry and Nelson, were equal partners in these cattle. I was to look after them while I also drew wages from Mr. Hall. By this time I was considered a very good stock hand as I was getting to be quite a man.

---

[1] Robert H. Hall came to the area in 1873 and went to work as the telegrapher at Camp Stambaugh, several miles north of Atlantic City. When the post was abandoned in 1878, he moved down to the Wind River Valley and got involved in the stock grazing business. In 1883 he homesteaded in what is now known as Lyons Valley.

[2] Worden P. Noble was a native of Sacketts Harbor, New York who came to Atlantic City as a freighter and merchant in 1868. He continued his freighting business until 1878, but began buying cattle in 1874. In 1880 he moved his cattle range from the Sweetwater to the Nowood. When he sold out his cattle operation in 1882 he had 7,000 head of cattle. Although he moved to Salt Lake City in 1883, he remained involved in mercantile, banking and stock grazing operations in central Wyoming for many years.

In 1881, after the spring roundup was over, I was stationed on the Overland Trail[3] just east of South Pass to inspect all cattle going through this country. I was known as the official trail inspector for this part of the country and my duties were to inspect all herds passing through to see that they did not take any of our cattle out of the country with them. This was quite frequently done.

There were lots of cattle trailing through here at this time, some of them going to their range in another part of Wyoming and some of them going to market.[4] It was not unusual at that time to see a herd of beef steers from Oregon that had been four months on the trail. They would be trailed as far as the feed was good and then shipped to market. I have spent two weeks going from one herd to another, living and sleeping with the trail herds.

As a rule, the boys were fine. When I would ride up to a herd I would tell the foreman who I was and what my business was. If he wished I would show him my credentials, which were complete and elaborate. I was very proud of them as they had been drawn up by an attorney in Cheyenne and had a big seal on them and were signed by all the cattlemen for which I was inspecting. I would ask them if they had any strays and usually

---

[3] Again, Farlow is referring to what we know as the Oregon-California Trail.

[4] Many cattle were brought to Oregon during the years that emigrant travel along the Oregon Trail was active. And by the late 1870s, there were enough cattle in that region to help stock the Rocky Mountain regions. The first herds coming from Oregon into Wyoming made the trip in 1876. By 1879, there were more than 100,000 cattle on the trail east each year. Many of these herds entered Wyoming in the Star Valley area and then followed the Lander Cutoff into the Sweetwater region. From the Sweetwater, cattle bound for Wyoming ranches headed off in many directions. Cattle which were to be shipped east were frequently moved to Rock Creek where they . were loaded on trains.

E.J. Farlow was joined in Wyoming by two of his brothers. This photograph is believed to show the three of them together in a Lander studio. Although identifications can not be confirmed, it is believed that E.J. Farlow is at left, Zeke Farlow is in the center, and Henry Farlow is at right. (Photo courtesy of Pioneer Museum, Lander)

they would tell me but sometimes leaving me to find out for myself. I was always asked to eat and sleep with them when I happened to be at their camp when night came.

⊠

In the hard winter of 1886 and '87, the cattle died by the thousands as there was absolutely no chance for them to be fed. They were to live on the range, the same as the buffalo.[5]

I was a cowboy in Wyoming that winter and was out among the cattle. Charles M. Russell was a cowboy in Montana. He was working for an eastern cattle syndicate that had just driven 5,000 head of Texas cattle onto their range. As the cattle were dying the eastern syndicate partners wrote often to their foreman in Montana as to conditions. One of their letters was handed to Russell to answer as he had just been out over the range. Russell was an artist so he drew a picture of an old, poor, skinny Texas cow, showing the company brand on it and in the distance a lone wolf waiting for his feed. The cow was standing in a foot of snow and under this Russell wrote, "The Last of Five Thousand?" He mailed it to them and this is the picture that made him famous.

He was a much better artist than cowboy.

---

[5] There is evidence that the winter of 1886-87 was not as severe in many parts of Wyoming as it was in Montana and the Dakotas. Although some counties—in the northwest part of the state—reported cattle losses as high as 80 percent, credible sources place the average loss across the state at not more than 15 percent.

THE LAMOREAUX FAMILY

I WAS STANDING ON THE sidewalk in Lander on April 28, 19—[1], talking to W.P. Noble, when Bill Lamoreaux came up and spoke, then walked away. Mr. Noble said, "I can tell you that boy's age and how he came by his name.

"His right name is Willow. In the early spring of 1868 we left Fort Laramie for South Pass. I was driving an ox team for Jules Lamoreaux. Jules was driving another and had his family in the wagon. His wife was Woman Dress, a full-blooded Sioux woman and the sister of war chief Gall, who led the Sioux in battle at Custer Massacre. His two children were Lizzie, four years old, and Dick, two years old.[2]

"There were 12 wagons, 17 men and three women. We were menaced by Indians on the Platte River near Casper but after a few shouts and shots they rode away. We traveled slowly as the

---

[1] Date is not legible on Farlow's original manuscript.

[2] Jules Lamoreaux learned the freighting business at Fort Laramie during the 1860s. It was there that he met and married Woman Dress in 1864. Upon his arrival in the South Pass area, he set up a tent store on the banks of Rock Creek in Atlantic City. Business went bad in 1870 and Lamoreaux returned to freighting, carrying goods between Point of Rocks on the Union Pacific and the mines. In 1874 he moved into the Wind River Valley and took up a homestead along the Middle Fork of the Popo Agie. He became one of the most successful of the early cattle men in the valley and served as Lander's second mayor.

Jules Lamoreaux died in 1914. Woman Dress died in 1908.

grass was short. Near Split Rock on Sweetwater, on what is now the McIntosh Ranch, we had traveled about an hour in the morning when Indians arose on all sides of us. We had driven right into an Indian trap. They began circling us on horseback and the arrows began falling thick and fast. We hastily corralled our wagons and prepared to defend ourselves.

"The shouts and war cries from the Indians came nearer as the circling Indians closed in on us, and it looked as if we were gone as they outnumbered us 20 to one.

"All at once Woman Dress recognized the voices as Sioux. She was a young, strong woman with a good voice and, coming out of the circled wagons, she began shouting to them in Sioux at the top of her lungs and going towards the Indians waving her blanket as she did so. As the Indians recognized her they ceased firing and shouted to her that they would come and talk to her if the white men would not fire at them. Through Jules Lamoreaux this message was passed on and the Indians, 12 of them, came riding up. Woman Dress talked to them and told them that she was a sister of Chief Gall and that her husband and children were with her and that if they were harmed Chief Gall would kill all of them. The Indians recognized her and rode away."[3]

Noble said that Woman Dress undoubtedly saved the lives of all in the train.

My wife Lizzie remembers the incident.[4] When the wagons were circled she wanted to peek out under the canvas to see

---

[3] Other accounts of this incident say that Woman Dress' brother Gall was a member of the raiding party.

[4] Elizabeth "Lizzie" Lamoreaux was the oldest daughter of Jules and Elizabeth (Woman Dress) Lamoreaux. She was born in 1864 at Fort Laramie. Educated at a Catholic convent at St. Hyacinth, Quebec, she was one of the belles of early Lander. Ed Farlow and Lizzie Lamoreaux were married in 1883. They had two sons—Jule and Albert (Stub). Lizzie Lamoreaux Farlow died in 1932.

what was going on. Her mother, Woman Dress, slapped her and made her and Dick lie in the wagon bed.

Noble continued, "We came on up Sweetwater and arrived at South Pass on the evening of April 27, 1868. The next morning Jules Lamoreaux came out of his tepee holding a new baby boy in his hands and said, 'See what happened last night.' He had named him Willow, because the tepee had been set under a bunch of willows."

WINTER ON RED DESERT

I N THE FALL OF 1881, after we gathered our beef, we trailed to Rawlins 135 miles for shipment as there was good feed all the way. We had ordered cars for our herd a month in advance so when we got to Rawlins we did not have to wait long for our cars.

It was very hard to get cars at that time. In the fall there were so many cattle demanding shipment that stockmen would sometimes wait a month for cars. There were five herds waiting near Rawlins for shipment.

Just before we shipped, there came up a very bad snow storm. It snowed and blowed for a day and a night and I was on herd all night. I was well dressed and had a good horse.

When I called the midnight guard he looked up at the snow and said "Let them go. I would not get out in this for all the cattle in Wyoming. You can't hold them anyhow."

I told him I had them yet and I rode back to the herd. I succeeded in getting them up under the shelter of a hill and held them until morning. A small bunch was split off but as soon as it came daylight we missed them and soon found them.

There was a trail herd of 1,250 head of beef from Oregon there and they lost all of them for three days and then found only half of them. After some time they found the balance and could not get cars. As these cattle were very poor and unfit to ship, the owner, a Mr. Hogsden, made a deal with Mr. Hall to take them to his range on the Beaver, winter them there, and ship them the next year.

After they got the cattle to the top of Beaver Hill and started them down towards the creek, Hogsden's outfit turned back and we had the cattle on our hands.

About the first of December, Mr. Hall decided he would go to Rawlins for a load of supplies and, taking a four-horse team, went and loaded out. Mr. Hogsden, still being in Rawlins, decided to come back with Hall and see for himself how the cattle were doing.

They got to Lost Soldier Creek, 42 miles from Rawlins, when another storm hit them and they lost their team. Hall left Mr. Hogsden at the camp with the loaded wagon and came to Beaver. He asked me if I had seen anything of the horses. I said "No." He then sent me with another team to get the wagon and bring it in. Hall met me on Sweetwater, took the team, and sent me back to look for the horses.

This was one of the hardest trips I ever made in my life. I had a good saddle horse and pack horse and I went back to Lost Soldier Creek. The snow was very deep and there was not a soul in 40 miles.[1]

After hunting a day there, I went west and struck a trail of four horses in the snow and followed them a day and got out on the Red Desert where the snow was not so deep. These tracks were headed for the Beaver country but were going around the west end of Crook Mountain. That night it snowed again and all tracks were lost.

---

[1] The road from Rawlins to Lander and Fort Washakie was still little more than a trail at this time. In the earliest days, travelers and freight came to South Pass, Lander and Fort Washakie from the Union Pacific Railroad at Bryan and Green River. But the route from Rawlins was significantly shorter. By 1880, the military had improved the trail to some extent and created a crude telegraph line. Soon thereafter a postal route was established along the road and with it came a stage line. It's likely the Lost Soldier stage station was soon established at or near the site where Hall and Hogsden camped and lost their team in 1881.

After hunting around there for two days, I started for the ranch. The next night I camped near Warm Springs on the south side of Sweetwater. The snow was about a foot deep and I would rustle sagebrush and clear the snow away and build a fire and cook my meals. They consisted of frying pan bread, bacon and coffee. I would then hobble my horses so they could not get away. I cut the end off my rope and put a second pair of rope hobbles on them. I then rolled up in my blankets and slept and rose till morning.

This night was the only night I had ever been afraid of wolves. It was very cold and they came around me and howled and sniffed; both wolves and coyotes. The night was dark and they came up to within about 50 feet of me. I was ready for them as I had a good Colt's .44 and was good with it. But they did not come close enough for me to get a good shot. I saw them dimly a time or two, but did not shoot. There were about a half a dozen of them but they sounded like a hundred.

The next day I made the ranch. The horses were found the next June on the Red Desert. I had been very near to them and had it not snowed, I am sure I would have soon found them. Even then I was good at trailing.

WINTER OF 1882-83 ON BEAVER

W HILE WORKING FOR Lamoreaux I lived in a dugout on Beaver, about ten miles south of Riverton. There were two dugouts and a small corral which had been built by fur trappers some years before.[1] My work was to keep water holes open for cattle and horses, and look after saddle horses along Beaver and on Wind River south of Riverton. My visitors were mostly Indians.

It was an open winter up to about February 1 when two feet of snow fell over the country. This was the storm in which Maggie Sherlock froze to death, and Al Dougherty froze his hands and feet, between South Pass and Big Sandy, north of Rock Springs.[2]

---

[1] Farlow apparently left the employ of R.H. Hall sometime between the winter of 1881-82 and the winter of 1882-83. Although Farlow locates his camp with reference to the town of Riverton, at the time Farlow camped there Riverton's birth was still more than 25 years in the future.

[2] The storm actually began on January 31, 1883. Maggie Sherlock, the 18-year-old daughter of Janet Smith of South Pass City, was on her way to attend school in Salt Lake City. Sherlock and George Ryder, the driver of the sleigh that was used as a stage during the winter, were stranded in the storm south of the Dry Sandy Stage Station for two nights and almost two days. Although both were found while still alive, they died later from the effects of their ordeal.

Another stage, driven by a man known only as Scott, left Pacific Springs for South Pass City on January 31. Scott and one of his passengers, William V. Clark of Lander, also died in the storm. A second passenger, W.J. Stuart

Reverend Roberts also came into the the country at that time.[3]

There were three herds of sheep camped along the Beaver that winter. Two were owned by a man named Haven, with Ed Gustin moving camp. One camped at Butler Crossing,[4] one at Red Hills, and Ed Earle and Frank Shedd[5] had their herd at the Big Bend of Beaver. By working hard, dragging trails with their team of horses, they saved about half their sheep. Haven lost most of his sheep and a lot of cattle died before spring.

---

survived the storm but was so badly frozen that he lost both hands, portions of both feet, his nose and both ears.

Al Dougherty was stranded in the same storm after leaving Big Sandy Station for Green River. He eventually lost one foot completely, and his other foot was amputated at the instep. Portions of most of his fingers on both hands were also amputated.

[3] Reverend John Roberts was a 30-year-old Episcopal priest embarking on a mission to the Shoshone Indian Reservation when he arrived in Green River on February 2, 1883. Within hours he was on his way north with the mail stage. When he arrived at the Dry Sandy Stage Station, he performed a burial service for George Ryder who had died in the storm that was still making its presence felt. When he arrived at Fort Washakie eight days after leaving Green River, he had completed a trip that normally took 36 hours. His work among the Indians on the reservation would continue for 66 years—the remainder of his life.

[4] Butler Crossing was named for Ed Butler. It was located near the point where Sand Draw empties into Beaver Creek in the area of the current Beaver Creek gas field.

[5] Edson A. Earle and Frank Shedd were homesteaders on the Little Popo Agie in what is now known as Lyons Valley. The Beaver Creek drainage was just over the ridge from their home places and it provided convenient grazing range for their sheep.

Working for a Squaw Man

J.L. Lamoreaux was what they called a "squaw man." He
was a Frenchman and had married a Sioux girl at old Fort
Laramie. He came to the mining district of South Pass
with his family in 1868 during the height of the gold rush. He
opened a store in Atlantic City and, in 1874, bought some cattle. He closed his store and moved to Lander Valley which was,
at that time, a wonderful cattle country. Being an Indian, he was
permitted to let his cattle run on the Indian reservation and that
led to my first real acquaintance with the Indians.[1]

I was in daily contact with the young Indians on the range
and friendships were formed then that continue to this day. Some
of the best and truest friends I have are those same Indians. From
them I have learned much of their past life and experiences.

We were camped down on the Big Popo Agie in July of
1883, after the roundup was over. I lost one of my saddle horses
and we hunted a week for him. One day a cowboy came into
camp and told me he had seen my horse in the Shoshone Indian
village just below the agency. The next morning, Smiling Fox[2]

---

[1] Jules Lamoreaux was not an Indian. He was of French-Canadian ancestry. However he was married to an Indian woman. That connection, apparently, gave him access to reservation lands which wasn't enjoyed by other
stockmen. Lamoreaux was out of the stock business by the late 1890s but he
ran a meat market in Lander for a number of years. He died in 1914.

[2] Smiling Fox was the Indian name of Willow Lamoreaux, second son of

and I saddled up a good horse each and went up there. There was my horse, picketed.

I rode up to him and put my rope over his neck and was just taking the Indian rope off when an Indian, My Cat Johnny, came out of a tepee nearby. He came running to me saying, "No, my horse, my horse."

I said, "No, my horse."

He came up and tried to take my rope off.

I told him not to but he kept trying. I had a heavy, shot-loaded quirt and wrapping the tail of it around my hand I hit him over the head, knocking him down. But I did not knock him out.

My Cat Johnny began to yell something in Shoshone and scrambled to his feet. He started for his tepee and his wife came out with his gun, which was an Army carbine. She handed it and a cartridge to him and he opened the breech block and dropped the cartridge in and started to raise the gun. As he looked up he was gazing squarely into the muzzle of my Colt's .44.

I said we would go see the Indian agent (I was well acquainted with him) and he said alright.

I motioned My Cat Johnny to walk ahead, which he did, and we started for the agency, which was but a short distance.

Soon someone rode up beside me. It was Henry Read, a Shoshone half-breed who I was also well acquainted with. Henry said to me, "Ed, put up your gun or they will kill you."

Looking around I saw about a dozen Shoshones with their guns.

We went to the agent's office and I told him of finding my horse and the Indian claiming it. I showed him a bill of sale that

---

Jules and Elizabeth Lamoreaux. Willow was also referred to at times as William or Bill.

I had from the man I bought it from. But My Cat Johnny said it was his horse and it had been stolen from him a year ago. That was about the time I bought it.

The agent, Dr. Irwin, was an old man and a good agent and he was satisfied that both of us were telling the truth. We fixed the matter up with him and then he said to me, "You had better let them have the horse or they will cause you a lot of trouble."

I did so and all was settled.

We had not told the agent of my hitting the Indian but when we came to the door of the office and looked out, there were about a hundred Shoshones lying along the edge of the brush and the road, each with a gun under his blanket. When Dr. Irwin saw this he said, "My God, boy, what have you done? Come back inside and I will send for the troops."

I did not know the Indians then as well as I do now, but I said, "No, we will go. I am not afraid."

He told me to ride off as quietly as possible and pay no attention to them and he would hold the door, meaning he would not let My Cat Johnny out to give any signal until I was gone.

Our horses were standing in front of the office with the reins down and we got on and rode off. You can bet I did not reach for my gun then.

The Indians beside the road eyed me like a snake and we had about a hundred yards to go before the road crossed Trout Creek where we would be behind the bushes.[3] As I neared this place a thought came to me: "Will I feel a bullet before I hear the shot?" I fully expected to be riddled.

---

[3] At the time, the Wind River Agency was located on Trout Creek, approximately half-way between what is now known as Hines' Corner and the Shoshone Episcopal Mission. The agency headquarters building was surrounded by houses for government employees. The little community which surrounded the agency was referred to for many years as Wind River.

When we got about 20 feet from the creek, I told Smiling Fox to lay low and "let's go." Stooping in the saddle, we put spurs to our horses and were out of sight.

After crossing the creek we kept close behind the willows and followed down the creek for about half a mile. Leaving the creek, we hit straight for Lander and we never stopped until we were safely off the reservation.

This was only a few years after the Meeker Massacre in Colorado and Mr. Irwin told me afterwards he fully expected to see me riddled with bullets. He sent the agency clerk to the fort which was a mile away[4] and the commanding officer came over with a company of soldiers and dispersed the Indians. There was great excitement for several days as My Cat Johnny was a medicine man and his dignity was considerably ruffled. I kept away from the Shoshones for some time after that.

I felt very badly over my trouble with the Shoshones and, as my work carried me among them quite often, I was somewhat afraid of more trouble some time later. As we were putting in an issue of beef at the agency slaughterhouse,[5] I went to the post

---

[4] Located on the Little Wind River, the military post which was at the site of current day Fort Washakie was established in 1871 when the buildings of the first Camp Brown were moved from the place which eventually became the town of Lander. This post was also referred to as Camp Brown until 1878 when it became Fort Washakie. The Bureau of Indian Affairs took over the post's buildings after the military abandoned it in 1909. Many of the military-era buildings still remain in use today.

[5] One of the difficulties faced by early Wind River Valley stock men was the lack of local markets for their beef. So competition for contracts to provide beef for the people of the Wind River Reservation was keen. The Wind River Agency purchased the beef for the Indians in partial fulfillment of the government's obligation to the tribes under the agreements that placed them on the reservation. Indian families gathered weekly at the reservation slaughterhouse to receive their issues of beef.

(Fort Washakie) where I saw my friend, the old scout and guide, William McCabe.[6] I told him of my trouble with My Cat Johnny and that I was sorry for what I had done. He said "We will go and see Washakie," which we did.[7]

When I told Washakie what I had done, he said he had heard about it.

I told him I was sorry for it and wanted to be friends with the Shoshones.

He smiled and took me by the hand and said that was good. He sent for My Cat Johnny. By the time he arrived there was quite a large gathering of Shoshones.

I told Johnny I was sorry for what I did and asked him to forgive me and be friends. I told him I believed it was his horse, but that I had bought it the past winter in Lander from a cowboy by the name of Ben Seaton. Some of them knew him and said he was no good. We shook hands and were again friends.

Washakie seemed greatly pleased and he later always called me his boy. He said that Dick (his son) and I were brothers and I was then and there accepted into the tribe as a brother.

---

[6] William McCabe had been in the Wind River country for many years and was one of the most knowledgeable and experienced of the area's frontiermen. Military officers at Fort Washakie utilized his services as a scout for many years.

[7] Washakie was the principal chief of the Eastern Shoshone Indians for many years. Born to a Flathead father and Shoshone mother sometime around 1800, he chose early to live with the Shoshones. Washakie began to emerge as a leader in the late 1840s and by the 1860s he was the dominant chief of the Eastern Shoshone. He was unique among Indian leaders in his early recognition that the survival of his people would require co-existence with the whites. In his later years he was widely respected by both Indians and whites for his wisdom and benevolence.

DIVISION OF THE SHOSHONES

THIS STORY WAS TOLD to me by the Shoshone interpreter Norkuk in the tepee of Washakie. There were also present several other prominent Indians whose names I do not remember at this late date. This story was told me in answer to my question as to how the Shoshones came to have this country. I had heard some talk by some of the older Indians that the Wind River Valley was disputed hunting grounds not so long ago.

Norkuk was a Shoshone Indian about fifty years old at that time and had spent some of his early life with Jim Bridger. He had learned to talk pretty good English. He was employed at the agency as an interpreter and had been in the Battle of Bear River.

He said the Shoshones were about twice as many as they were now and that 14 snows gone by (meaning 14 years ago) they were camped on Green River on the west side of the Rocky Mountains about 30 miles from the old emigrant road. They had been robbing the emigrants, stealing their horses and cattle, and burning their wagons and had been very successful that year. They had just returned to camp from a successful raid and were having a big dance and council talk by the older Indians when one of their scouts came in from Fort Bridger with some of the wounded from their last raid, which was on five wagons about 25 miles from Fort Bridger. The scout said some soldiers were there and they were pretty mad and that the "Big

Chief," meaning General Connor,[1] was going to try and punish the Indians.

In the tribe at this time were three prominent chiefs—Old Sagwitch, Bear Hunter, and Washakie. Washakie was the youngest of the three. After some talk he got up and said "We had better leave the white people alone and let us all go to the Wind River Valley. There we will have plenty of buffalo, deer, elk, antelope, lots of beaver and fish in the streams, lots of wood and we will be happy and will disturb no one."

Old Bear Hunter got up and said the white man had to be robbed and killed and their stock stolen and the Shoshones might as well do it as let the Sioux or Arapahoes do it. He intimated that Washakie was afraid.

Washakie arose and cast his blanket on the ground and drawing his knife he stepped out and said "If there is anyone here that thinks Washakie is afraid, let him stand forth."

And no one moving, he continued. "If there are any two men here that think Washakie is afraid let them meet me now or say no more."

Bear Hunter very wisely held his peace.

Washakie continued, "I am going to take my family and go into the Wind River Valley and let the white man alone and all those that care to follow me I will be glad to have."

About half the Indians drew apart and went with Washakie and came into the Wind River Valley.

The rest of the tribe under Sagwitch and Bear Hunter moved their winter camp on Bear River in southwest Wyoming. That winter—in January—the camp on Bear River was attacked by General Connor and his troops and most of the Shoshone men were either killed or wounded. Norkuk said they were attacked in the morning. It was a very cold day with lots of

---

[1] General Patrick E. Connor.

snow on the ground and they were driven into the river. As he was crossing the river, keeping as low in the water as he could, a bullet from a soldier's gun tore out one eye. Hence his name, Norkuk, meaning one-eyed man. He said he was heap scared.

General Connor's report shows about 250 dead Indians and he says the soldiers took no prisoners. He says they secured about 175 ponies and a large amount of supplies. They burned about 75 lodges and left about 140 women and children unmolested after destroying their homes, burning all their bedding and provisions, and killing and wounding all their men. Connor left them to starve and freeze to death.[2]

The survivors of this battle made their way to Fort Bridger, as old Jim Bridger was the only friend they could think of in their terrible plight. Sagwitch, Bear Hunter and another chief called Leight were all killed.

I have talked with some of the survivors of this fight and they say that many more of them died from cold or hunger.

The remnants of this band are now called Bannocks and are on the Fort Hall Indian Reservation on the Snake River in Idaho.

---

[2] The Battle of Bear River took place on January 29, 1863. Farlow's account is faithful to other reports of the battle. However, some other sources set the number of Indians killed at close to 400. Other reports indicate also that Connor did leave the surviving women and children with some provisions.

BATTLE OF CROWHEART BUTTE

Washakie and his followers came into the Wind River Valley and lived in peace and plenty until the following July. Then, upon arising one morning, they discovered a large war party of about 100 Crow Indians driving off a large bunch of their horses. Washakie's men mounted as quickly as possible and gave chase. Following them to Big Wind River the Shoshones found the Crows were heading for a ford farther up the river, the river being quite high. The Crows did not know there was a ford just below them.

The Shoshones divided. Part of them crossed at the lower ford and went up the other side to cut the Crows off, which they soon did. And with the other band of Shoshones pressing in closely from behind, the Crows abandoned the stolen horses and took refuge on a very large butte rising above the surrounding country.

The butte is a landmark for many miles around and it is almost inaccessible. The top of the butte is almost flat and has an area of about an acre. Once the Crows were upon it, they could easily hold the Shoshones at bay.

The chief of the Crows, Big Robber, being a mighty warrior, shouted defiance to the Shoshones and dared them to send a man against him. Washakie was for going up and fighting him, but the other Indians said "No, we will starve them out."

The next day the Crow chief again shouted his defiance and dared the Shoshone chief to come up and fight him. Washakie could stand his taunts no longer and, standing erect, he signaled he would come up. He climbed the side of the butte and stood on the edge.

Facing the Crows, Washakie said "I have come at the bidding of your chief to fight him. You are many. I am one. You can easily kill me, but if you do, not one of you will leave here alive. So my people will know of this fight I will call the Shoshones to the top also so they may see that it is fair. And as the Crows also claim this valley, this fight shall decide who shall have it. The one that loses will go away and never claim this country again."

The Crows said it was good and the Shoshones came to the top of the butte.

The two men drew apart and then Washakie slew his enemy. The rest of the Crows departed, went north, and never came back.

I fix the time of this battle in 1865 as the battle of Bear River was in '64.[1]

The Shoshones made a treaty with the U.S. government in 1868 for this valley and have been peaceable Indians ever since.

---

[1] The Battle of Bear River took place in January of 1863. But the date of the Crowheart Butte incident cannot be placed with certainty. Edmo LeClair is said to have placed it in March of 1866 but other sources contradict that claim. Virginia Trenholm and Maurine Carley in their history *The Shoshonis* place it sometime between the fall of 1858 and the spring of 1859.

The exact sequence of events is also uncertain. Trenholm and Carley say the climactic duel on the butte took place after four days of battle between the Shoshones and the Crows. And what did Washakie do after killing Big Robber? One account says Washakie cut out his heart and displayed it on his lance. Another story says he ate Big Robber's heart.

It's unlikely that we'll ever be able to separate fact from legend but it is apparent that Washakie's victory convinced the Crow Indians to stay out of the Wind River Valley and concede it as Shoshone territory.

HARVEY MORGAN

I N JUNE, 1870 OLD Major Kuykendall, in command of 80 men and two mountain howitzers drawn by oxen, camped on the Little Popo Agie River about ten miles from Camp Brown on the Big Popo Agie. At noon on the 27th of June there arrived in the Major's camp six men—three in a wagon (Doc Barr, Jerome Mason, and Harvey Morgan[1]) and three on horseback (E.F. Cheney, Charles Oldham and John Anthony). These men stopped and had dinner with some friends they found in the camp. This command was made up of one company of regular U.S. soldiers and about 20 miners, trappers and prospectors who had availed themselves of this opportunity of getting safe conduct through this dangerous country.[2]

After dinner, the three men with the wagon hitched up their team and started for Camp Brown. Just before they started the Major said to them, "Boys don't go. I can see Indians in these hills with glasses."

---

[1] Dr. R.S. Barr lived in South Pass City and served as a Justice of the Peace. Morgan had a ranch on the lower North Fork of the Popo Agie.

[2] A series of attacks on whites by Indians during the spring of 1870 in the South Pass and Wind River Valley areas made everyone nervous. Among the casualties was Lieutenant Charles Stambaugh who was killed near Miner's Delight on May 4, 1870. As a result of these incidents, General C.C. Augur issued orders on June 20 for the establishment of a new military post in the South Pass area. That post later became known as Camp Stambaugh.

Harvey Morgan spoke up and said he was not afraid of all the damn Indians in the country "with old Betsy here," and he patted a new Henry repeating rifle he had.

The other three men stayed and had supper in camp and then saddled up and started for Camp Brown.

Going for about four miles and coming to the top of a ridge, Cheney, Oldham and Anthony discovered on the next ridge ahead of them in the darkness what looked like a wagon. Immediately dropping behind the ridge they went to the right, keeping behind the ridge until they came to a gulch that ran near the ridge on which they had seen the wagon. They followed the very bottom of the gulch until they were very near the wagon.

E.F. Cheney later said, "We left John Anthony to hold the horses and Oldham and I crawled up toward the wagon, stopping now and then to listen. Not a sound could we hear. By this time it was getting quite dark."

Cheney, putting his hand in something damp, whispered to Oldham, "I believe I have put my hand in some blood." Cheney, being a butcher, knew the feel of blood.

Oldham struck a match and as it flared up it showed Cheney's hand red with blood. And there, not more than a yard away, was a dead body. They at once retraced their steps and, mounting their horses, very cautiously made their way to Camp Brown where they reported what they had found.

The next morning the commanding officer at the post sent a detachment of soldiers to the scene of the killing.[3] Cheney piloted the troops to the scene. He says their wagon was stopped in a

---

[3] The site of the killing can no longer be pinpointed precisely but it was somewhere near the route of Highway 287, approximately six miles southeast of Lander. A monument erected in memory of the three men stands next to the highway as it passes through what is now known as Deadman Gulch.

big wolf den, the box and front bolster being on the ground, the wagon badly shot up. It looked as if the boys had made a grand fight and held the Indians at bay until their ammunition was gone. When the Indians came up and killed them the ground was literally packed down around the scene of battle by thousands of moccasin tracks. The Indians had ridden in a circle around the whites while fighting and had a beaten track. There seems to have been a large war party.

After the Indians had killed the whites they scalped Jerome Mason and Harvey Morgan. Then they cut the skin across the back of Morgan's neck and split the skin down the entire length of his back and skinned it back about four inches on each side. They took out the sinews of his back. Cheney says Morgan's back was terribly mutilated. The Indians then drove the wagon hammer through Morgan's head using the neck yoke. Cheney says he is satisfied this was the last act as the hammer had some red paint on it which came from the neck yoke.[4]

The bodies were taken to Camp Brown and buried on the bank of the stream. The grave of Morgan was eventually lost. In 1912, while workmen were digging a water line in Lander, the bones of Morgan were found with the the wagon hammer in his skull. The skull is now in the possession of the Fremont County Pioneer Association.[5]

---

[4] H.G. Nickerson wrote later that the party of Indians who attacked Barr, Mason and Morgan were Arapahos numbering about 200. He noted that Morgan's treatment was particularly heinous in view of the fact that he was well known to the Arapahos and had frequently fed and befriended them. After killing Barr, Mason and Morgan, the group of Indians went on to attack W.A. Barrett at his ranch in Red Canyon (Barrett was able to stand them off and escape injury), and then to South Pass where they stole 200 horses. Nickerson said the group was pursued without success by Lieutenant Robinson and a company of the 2nd Cavalry.

[5] The skull is on display at the Pioneer Museum in Lander.

The finding of these bodies and the official reports of both Major Kuykendall and the commander of Camp Brown are on file with the War Department in Washington D.C. The major arrived on the scene the next morning at the same time as the commander from the post. The bodies, the wagon, and the grounds were carefully investigated and both officers made report of what they found.

Harvey Morgan's skull is one of the strangest relics in existence of Indian hatred and vindictiveness, and shows the hatred existing at that time against the invasion of the white man in Indian country.

LIZZIE LAMOREAUX FARLOW

I N ABOUT OCTOBER OF 1881 Den Crowley and I were looking for cattle for George East when I woke up one morning
with mountain fever. I knew Mrs. Gillis very well so I came
to the Gillis home in Lander. Lizzie Lamoreaux was also a very
good friend of Mrs. Gillis and the next day she came to visit. I
was a pretty hard looker, not having shaved for a couple of
months and burning with fever. Lizzie expected to see a very nice
young man as she had heard a lot about me from Mrs. Gillis. So
she was disgusted with my appearance. That was the first time I
saw my future wife, a very good-looking half-blood Sioux girl.[1]

The doctor from Fort Washakie came over to see Wilbur
Iiams and so Mrs. Gillis called him in for me. He prescribed for
me and I soon broke the fever and got well.

About a year later a young Catholic priest named Father
Moriarity arrived in Lander by stage. Captain H. G. Nickerson,
Cotton Hook Jackson, two others and myself went over to meet
the stage. Jackson met the priest with insulting language.

"Hello Deacon," Jackson said. "Where in hell did you come
from?"

---

[1] This doesn't ring true. Earlier Farlow has talked about working for Jules
Lamoreaux and his friendship with the Lamoreaux boys. Is it conceivable
that he would be meeting Lizzie for the first time somewhere other than at
the Lamoreaux home? And is it conceivable that she would have heard of
Farlow from Mrs. Gillis rather than from Mr. Lamoreaux or his sons?

Although it cannot be confirmed, this photograph is believed to show E.J. Farlow and Elizabeth Lamoreaux shortly after they were married in Lander. (Photo courtesy of Pioneer Museum, Lander.)

Father Moriarity simply extended his hand and smiled as he said, "Hello, Bill, where in hell do you live?"

This completely dismayed the tough Jackson.

Father Moriarity held services and invited all to come to church. Lamoreaux was a Catholic and his daughter Lizzie went regularly to church. She became a devout Catholic for the rest of her life.

In order to raise funds for a church in Lander, there being none at that time, Father Moriarity put on a Catholic fair.[2] A cow was raffled off (it had been donated by Henry Harting) and it brought $100. Another $82 was brought in at a dance on Christmas Eve. A gold-headed cane was offered to the most popular man. Votes were purchased for 10 cents each. The cane was won by Ike Bowman and the contest brought in $40.

A gold watch was offered as the prize in the most popular girl contest. Lizzie Lamoreaux and Ella McCarty were nominated.[3] Ella was an Irish girl and related to the O'Briens, the Crowleys and W. P. Noble. This split the town into two sections—the Moccasin Band and the Irish Brigade. W. P. Noble led the Irish vote and Jules Lamoreaux led the Indian vote. They were the biggest cattlemen in the valley. Votes were marked on a blackboard as they were purchased. Excitement ran high, but the Irish Brigade finally decided that the Indians didn't know when to quit and so Lizzie Lamoreaux won the watch. The watch brought $1,185—the highest price ever paid for a watch in Lander.

---

[2] Father Daniel W. Moriarity had just been ordained when he came to Lander in 1882. His efforts to build a church were aided by a substantial gift from Eugene Amoretti, Sr. The church was completed in 1883 and remained in use at the corner of 3rd and Garfield until 1920. A stone building at the sight was dedicated in 1928.

[3] Other accounts refer to Miss McCarty as Molly.

THE PRESIDENT'S TRIP

IN THE EARLY DAYS we got our mail by stage from Green River, a town on the Union Pacific Railroad, 150 miles from Lander. There was a daily stage which left Green River each morning at seven A.M. Another stage left Fort Washakie at the same time and it took these stages 36 hours to make the trip through, averaging about seven miles an hour, exclusive of stops. The stage stations were about fifteen miles apart as near as could be arranged.

At each of these stations the stages would stop and change horses. Some of stations were also eating places.

It was an endurance contest to ride one of these stages through in those days, 36 hours of bouncing and jolting without stopping except for meals and to change horses.

There were three drivers each way; each driver going three stations. Green River Station was 15 miles from Green River City. Then there was Alkali; so called for it was on alkali spring. They had to haul water for drinking. Starvation station was on a desert and they had to haul both wood and water—water for their horses as well as the men. I remember a sign there that read: Wood–40 miles; Water–20 miles; Grass–None; Hell–Right here.

At Big Sandy, the home station, stages stopped for meals and there were a lot of extra horses kept there. There was also a blacksmith shop and supplies for the line.

Other stations were Little Sandy, Pacific Springs, South Pass, Red Canyon, Lander and Fort Washakie (called Camp

Brown until January 1, 1880 when the name was changed to Fort Washakie[1]).

In 1883 we read in the papers about the proposed trip of President Chester Arthur, giving his proposed route through our little town of Lander. The papers were full of it. The President of the United States was going to risk his life by penetrating into the very heart of Indian country to investigate conditions for himself and also to see the great Yellowstone National Park. Troops were brought from Fort Russell, Camp Carlin, Fort Sanders, Fort Steele, and Fort Washakie and a detachment was stationed at each stage station along the entire route. I think in all there were nearly 2,000 troops on the line.

The President and his party (which consisted of Robert Lincoln, General Phil Sheridan, General Sherman and others I do not remember; eight in all[2]) left Green River City in two government ambulances. Each was drawn by four fine mules and escorted by about 100 mounted troops. This escort and the teams on the ambulances were changed at each station.

The party stopped the first night at a specially arranged camp on Little Sandy, the next day making Fort Washakie. There was no more danger then than now. The stages were running each day, and people were living at the mines[3] and in the Lander valley.

At Fort Washakie the presidential party rested for three days and inspected the Indians. There were at this time nearly 2,000

---

[1] The name change became official on January 1, 1878.

[2] General W.T. Sherman was not a part of President Arthur's party. The president's official party did include Governor Schuyler Crosby of Montana, General P.H. Sheridan, General Anson Stager, Judge Dan G. Rollins of New York, Secretary of War Robert T. Lincoln, and Senator George C. Vest of Missouri.

[3] Farlow refers here to the Sweetwater mines in and around South Pass City, Atlantic City and Miners Delight. Following the initial boom of the

Indians on this reservation. The Shoshones under the great Chief Washakie numbering nearly 1,000, and the Arapahos under Chief Black Coal nearly the same number. The Indians put on a sham battle and a big wolf dance for the benefit of their distinguished visitors. Washakie, at the close of the dance, presented the President with a handsome pinto Indian pony. The President thanked the Chief in a very nice speech which was very carefully interpreted to the Indians. In return the President made another nice talk and presented Chief Washakie with a gorgeously colored Indian blanket and the Chief's eyes sparked with admiration. Receiving the blanket he laid it across his arm and stroked it fondly. Then, for almost a minute, he stood very meekly in an attitude of devotion. He stood quietly for so long a time that his old friend J.K. Moore, who stood beside him, nudged him and told him to say something to thank the great White Chief.

Washakie slowly raised his head and said, "Washakie no good talk. Washakie's heart talks to great white chief. Washakie's heart says he is glad, and asks Great Spirit to bless white chief and make his heart good toward the Indian."

This, when interpreted to the President, affected him very much and he remarked he had never heard a better or more impressive speech of acceptance in his life.

From there the entire party went on horseback, escorted by many troops and a pack train of nearly two hundred mules. They went up Wind River, over the Continental Divide, down the Gros Ventre to Snake River, up Snake River and Jackson Lake to the crossing of Snake River and the park line, 175

---

late 1860s and early '70s, the population of this area had dropped drastically. The press correspondent who traveled with the presidential party described South Pass City and Atlantic City as virtually deserted. He reported there were a few working miners living at Miner's Delight.

miles from Fort Washakie. There a military escort met them from Fort Yellowstone and escorted them through the famous Yellowstone National Park and to their station on the Northern Pacific Railroad where the presidential party entrained for the east.

SACAJAWEA

W HEN I FIRST CAME among the Shoshones there was pointed out to me a very old woman who Norkuk said was Sacajawea. But that is not the name he called her and that is not the name she went by here.

Norkuk said that Sacajawea and her husband Toussaint,[1] as he called him, went with a party of white men a long time ago to the west, over the mountains and on west to the Big Water. He said she told about seeing a fish there that was as long as four tepee poles and was taller than she was. Norkuk asked me if that could be as the Indians did not believe it.

I told him I had never seen one that big but had read of them in books and that it was true fish in the Big Water grew that big.

There were also with the Shoshones at that time—1881— two warriors called Baptiste and Basil (pronounced Bazille). They were said to be her sons. I knew them both and was well acquainted with Basil. His boy Andrew and I were about the same age and used to be together. He had a racing pony and one of the first races I ran with the Indians was against this pony. My horse got beat. This race was a half-mile for one dollar. I lost the dollar and Andrew was well pleased. I laughed and took my defeat good-naturedly.

I was telling Senator Kendrick of these events a few years ago and showed him the grave of Sacajawea in the Indian graveyard

---

[1] Toussaint Charbonneau

near the agency. The old timers here had put up a small monument and marked it.

Senator Kendrick said it deserves a better marking than that. "I will introduce a bill in Congress for a monument as this is of national importance."

This he did.

Later, he was surprised to find that other stories had Sacajawea buried somewhere on the Missouri River in Dakota. The senator from that state made objection to Senator Kendrick's proposal and the matter stopped.[2]

Senator Kendrick wrote to me for additional evidence that this was Sacajawea who was buried here. There also came here a Dr. Eastman, an educated Sioux Indian and an inspector for the Indian Department, and he investigated thoroughly.[3]

Reverend Roberts officiated at Sacajawea's funeral. She was one of the first Indians who were buried here with the white man's services.

We dug up the body of old Basil. My friend Andrew said he saw his father wear a medal that was the property of his grandmother and was sure it was buried with his father. We did not

---

[2] Those who believe Sacajawea is buried elsewhere point to several items of documentary evidence. Breckenridge mentions her in his 1811 journal when he was traveling up the Missouri River from St. Louis. "We have on board," he writes, "a Frenchman named Charbonet, who with his wife, an Indian woman of the Snake nation, both of whom accompanied Lewis and Clark to the Pacific.... She has become sickly and longed to revisit her native country."

Then on December 12, 1812, a man at Fort Manuel on the upper Missouri River wrote in his journal that "the wife of Charbonneau, a Snake Squaw, died this evening of putrid fever, she was good and the best woman in the fort; aged about twenty-five years."

[3] Charles Eastman was a Sioux Indian, a physician, author and a noted lecturer. He was commissioned by the Indian Department in December of

find it but we found a wallet that appeared to contain official papers. When the papers were exposed to the air and light they crumbled to dust and we could not make out a single word. Basil had been buried forty years in a damp place and was well rotted to pieces.[4]

In talking with the older Indians who knew Sacajawea, they are sure she is the woman who piloted the Lewis and Clark expedition to the Pacific coast in 1805 and 1806. But we have been unable to find one word of written evidence. All they know is that this woman came back to them in the early 1840s with her two sons—then men—and a Comanche husband. She had been gone nearly 40 years and was recognized and accepted by her brother and relatives. Her age and appearance tallies exactly with the Sacajawea of the Lewis and Clark fame. Her two sons, Baptiste and Basil, tally exactly in age and appearance with the two sons she had when she disappeared earlier from history.

She told of leaving the Indians and of finding the Comanches. They are a part of the old Snake tribe. They and the Bannocks

---

1924 to conduct a study to determine the burial place of Sacajawea. He conducted interviews with Indians in Oklahoma, Wyoming and North Dakota and concluded that "Sacajawea, after sixty years of wandering from her own tribe, returned to her people at Fort Bridger and lived the remainder of her life with her sons in peace until she died on April 9, 1884, at Fort Washakie, Wyoming."

[4] Basil (or Bazil) died in 1886. His body was wrapped in a sheet and taken up Mill Creek where it was placed under the crumbling bank of a gulch. In 1924, Andrew Basil helped locate his father's grave in an effort to retrieve a wallet of important papers that had been buried with him. Reverend Roberts' son later wrote that the wallet was found but the "contents had been so ruined by moisture and the passage of time that nothing could be deciphered."

In 1939, a group led by archeologist Dr. Eugene Sterling and Works Progress Administration engineer Albert S. Parks dug in an effort to find Baptiste's body. Newspaper accounts do not indicate if that group had any success.

and Shoshones are all one and the same tribe—all descended from the old Snake Indians. They speak the same language and look the same.

In 1864 she came into this valley with Washakie and lived and died here, as did her two sons. Andrew is the only grandson living. Jessee Bay, a Shoshone, is a great-grandson of hers, being a grandson of Baptiste.[5]

The medal we were hunting for is supposed to be one of six given to Charbonneau by Captain Lewis and by Charbonneau to his wife. If this could be found it would undoubtedly identify Sacajawea. Andrew says he has seen his Father wear it many times when he would dress up for dances or for council meetings. But he does not know what was on it. He said there was a man on it and that is all he knows.

Baptiste died in 1884, I think, and was buried in the sliding rocks on a small cottonwood creek. Andrew thinks he can find him and we thought of digging him up to see if we could find anything. But Andrew thinks he saw his father wear it after Baptiste was dead. So I think we will not try anymore to establish the identity of Sacajawea. We know she is buried here and that is enough.

---

[5] Baptiste's son—Wyt-to-gan—told Reverend Roberts that his father had talked often about being carried on his mother's back when she led the "first Washington" across the mountains to the Great Waters and toward the setting sun.

VOTING AT RONGIS

I T WAS THE FALL OF 1884 and the beef roundup was over. I was living on a ranch near Lander and I had my crop put away. I and a man by the name of John Gillis rigged up two eight-horse teams and went to Rawlins for a load of freight—some for ourselves and some for the merchants and saloons in Lander.

On our return trip we drove all day without stopping for dinner in order to get in to a voting precinct in Fremont County to vote. This was the first general election in Fremont County. The county had just been organized out of the north end of Sweetwater County.[1] John Gillis and I were coming from Rawlins, each with a load of freight.

About 4 o'clock we drove up in front of the saloon at Rongis and the voting population of the precinct came pouring out of the saloon to greet us. They were filled with politics, enthusiasm

---

[1] The Wyoming territorial legislature approved an act establishing Fremont County on March 5, 1884. The first election was held on April 22, 1884. The first general election was held that fall.

Fremont County had been a part of Sweetwater County, which stretched from Wyoming's southern border to the northern border. People in the South Pass area and in the Wind River Valley felt they were too far removed from the county seat at Green River and so efforts to establish a new county were initiated. That new county included most of what we know today as Sublette County, Hot Springs County, Park County, and portions of Big Horn and Washakie counties.

and Johnny Signor's whiskey. They told us we had to come in and have a drink even before we unhitched.

None of them had voted yet. There were 15 of them, and we made 17.

We turned the horses loose and talked politics for a short time and had another drink on Cheeko, an outlaw who was electioneering for Jim Atkins, a candidate for sheriff. Cheeko had been busy all day with the bunch and had converted all of them, except for one little old man that had been cooking for the 71 outfit at Three Crossings on Sweetwater, about 10 miles down the river.

Rongis was on the Sweetwater River and was named by spelling the name of the owner—Signor—backwards. It consisted of three log cabins—one for the saloon, one for the kitchen and dining room, and one for the bunkhouse.[2]

As Jim Atkins was a warm, personal friend of mine, I was all right with Cheeko.

Just before going in to supper, a man there who knew all about elections said "Boys, we had better vote before we go." So they stopped the poker game that was going, cleared off the table and sat the ballot box on it. The judges opened the box to

---

[2] Rongis was a notable stopping place on the Rawlins–Lander road for many years. John J. Signor first established his ranch on the Sweetwater in the late 1870s. Across the river was the Elkhorn Post and Telegraph Office. But the post office was soon moved over to Signor's place and it became known as Rongis. Other sources say there was a two-story building at Rongis along with a post office, a store, and a blacksmith shop. Stage company use of the Rawlins–Lander road ended in 1906 but Rongis remained a post office until 1916.

The site of Rongis is still identifiable by the remains of several buildings. A bottle dump helps identify the location of the old saloon. That saloon remains in existence on the Whitlock Ranch, about one mile east of the old Rongis site.

show it was empty and then closed and locked it. We put our ballots in through a hole in the top.

This was before the days of the secret ballot and we were showing our ballots freely to each other. But after supper Cheeko suggested we had better open the box and see if all had voted right. The man who knew all about elections said that no one but the judges had a right to touch that box. So they got the judges, unlocked the box, poured the ballots out on the table and counted them. There were 18 of them. There were only 17 voters and so considerable discussion was indulged in as to the extra ballot. It was finally decided to let it alone as it was impossible to tell which ballot it was.

One man had not voted for Jim Atkins, but had voted for his opponent. Cheeko, straightening up and looking around, spied the little old man sitting on a beer keg in the corner. Walking over to him Cheeko took him by the ear and marched him up to the table. Pointing an accusing finger at the offending ballot, Cheeko sternly said "Is that your vote?"

The little man said it was.

"Tear it up," said Cheeko.

The old man did.

Handing him another ballot Cheeko told him to vote it right, which he did. It was put in the box with the rest. Cheeko, muttering and cursing the little man, said, "What do you mean? Are you trying to queer this election? Do you want to throw this whole precinct out?"

After this was all settled Cheeko turned to the old man and said, "Now to show you there are no hard feelings in this matter, we will let you buy the drinks for the crowd."

This the old man did and all was well.

The next morning the judges got a cowboy who was out of a job to carry the ballot box to Lander, a distance of 65 miles.

Johnny Signor loaned him a horse as he was broke. Johnny also loaned him a saddle and gave him $10 for expenses. They fixed up a bill that he was to deliver to the county clerk along with the ballot box.

Three weeks later the returns were all in except for the Rongis ballot box and the votes were counted. The Rongis ballots never got in. Nor did Signor ever see his horse and saddle again.

The next spring on the Sweetwater roundup, some of the boys found the box about two miles from Rongis where it had been thrown in the bottom of a gulch.

Jim Atkins was elected Sheriff just the same.[3]

---

[3] James J. Atkins was a native of Wisconsin who raised cattle in the Wind River Valley. He garnered 285 votes in the 1884 election to 247 for B.F. Lowe and 179 for Nelson Yarnell. Atkins took office in January of 1885. He served until January of 1887 and eventually was involved in several mining ventures in the Lewiston area.

It's important to note that Atkins was not the first sheriff of Fremont County. B.F. Lowe was elected to that post in the special election held in the spring of 1884 and he served as sheriff until Atkins took office.

BILL JEWELL

I N THE SUMMER OF 1885 I was working for the OX and L outfits. A young Montana cowboy named Bill Jewell also worked for these outfits that summer.

Around October Bill rode into the big corral at the L outfit's headquarters below where Hudson now stands and stayed all night. He was a very proud young man, did not drink or smoke, did not gamble, had a good bank roll and a fine horse. His saddle had his initials engraved on the back.

Bill was on his way back to Montana and wanted to buy some Indian ponies to take back. At that time they were plentiful and very cheap. He asked me where he could get them and I told him to go to Sharp Nose's camp at the mouth of Mill Creek. Sharp Nose was the war chief of the Arapahos. Bill intimated to me at that time that he had about $500 in cash with him.

He left the next morning for Sharp Nose's camp and that was the last time I ever saw him.

Later, while delivering beef at Fort Washakie, I saw Sharp Nose riding Bill Jewell's horse.

I turned to the old scout Bill McCabe and said, "That is Bill Jewell's horse."

"Are you sure?" he asked.

"I am positive," I said. "I worked with him all summer on the OX and L outfits. He told me that he would never sell that horse."

McCabe said, "Well, take a good look and make sure you are right."

I did and I noticed that the initials on the back of the saddle had been scratched off.

McCabe said something crooked had been going on. Sharp Nose and Garfield Wolf had plenty of money lately.

This was all reported to the commander at the fort and he sent a small detachment of troops with McCabe to Sharp Nose's camp. There McCabe found that the Indians were afraid of a certain slough there as they were very superstitious. In this slough they found a man's body. He had been shot twice through the body and scalped. He had also been stripped of most of his clothes. The body was taken to the fort and buried. Sharp Nose and Garfield Wolf were arrested and charged with murder. When confronted with the evidence they admitted the killing but said that Bill Jewell had come there drunk and wanted to fight. They said they had killed him in self defense.

They were sentenced and sent to the penitentiary for six to ten years.

When I heard they had found the body I asked Tom Spoonhunter where the scalp was and he got it for me from Sharp Nose's tepee.

HOW I BECAME A MEDICINE MAN

I T WAS IN THE FALL of 1885, I believe, that we were camped on the Big Wind River, about 10 miles below where the town of Riverton now stands. We had been out for a month gathering beef for shipment and were nearly through. We had a herd of about a thousand big steers and dry cows.

The outfit consisted of a pool wagon. A pool wagon is used when two or three small outfits throw in together and send out only one wagon and a cook, and a day and night horse wrangler. In this case the L, the Half Circle Cross, and the Double Wrench brands were working together and there were seventeen cowboys.

By standing night guard in pairs we were left with one odd man. So I had been standing two guards in order to even it up. I had stood the last half of the night before. On this evening the cattle were bedded on a sagebrush flat not far from the wagon. The night came on dark and threatening. It was a big storm and the cattle were restless. At 10 o'clock, when the second guard was called, it was so dark one could not see a foot except when there was a flash of lightning. It was an electric storm and the first guard remained to help the second hold the cattle as great drops of rain began to fall. There were blinding flashes of lightning followed by deafening claps of thunder and the cattle were milling. It looked very much like a bad stampede.

The night horse wrangler was holding the saddle horses nearby. It being his first experience of this kind, he was watching

90

to see what was done. His name was Nocksonna, an Arapaho. Interpreted into English, Nocksonna meant Buckskin.

Red Fox,[1] a brother of Smiling Fox, was on guard and soon after the second guard came on he told Nocksonna to go to camp and call Wa Wee Nacha, meaning me. Wa Wee Nacha interpreted into English means Working Chief.

Now Nocksonna knew that I had been on the last night and it was not my turn to be called. In fact every other man should be called first, and he wondered why I was to be called. He came to my bed and I was ready to go. I thought it was time for me, and my horse was always saddled.

I will say here that for ten years while working on the roundups, my saddle was always on a good horse night and day and I was always ready to go if needed. I carried eight head of good horses in my string.

I was out to the herd almost as soon as the Indian and could see nothing. The cattle were milling and bellowing and nervous. I can only liken them to a team of horses that have become frightened and are up on the bit ready to run at the slightest cause. The wonder to me is that the cattle did not go.

Waiting for a flash in order to see them, I could see that the men did not know if they were outside of all the cattle or not and they were scared of a stampede, for they are very dangerous to both men and beast. I had been in just such a situation before and knew what to do. I find that about all there is to this world is to know what to do at the right time.

I rode into the middle of the herd and, finding a pretty good patch of sagebrush, got off and built a fire. My horse stood there with reins down. I moved carefully so as not to frighten the cattle

---

[1] Smiling Fox was Will Lamoreaux, son of Jules Lamoreaux. However, it is not clear which of Will Lamoreaux' brothers was known as Red Fox—Richard, George, or Oliver.

and kept on feeding the fire. The flames mounted high as my head. The cattle were attracted by the fire and the boys could see everything between them and the fire and soon got to circling the cattle in an orderly way. After a few more flashes and crashes and roars, and a few more big drops of rain, the storm began to subside. The lightning grew less bright and the thunder grew less. The clouds began drifting away and soon a star appeared.

All this time I was feeding the fire. I think I was about 45 minutes with this fire. Looking about me I could see the cattle had become quiet and one or two were lying down. The sight of the fire had attracted their attention from the storm and soothed them. I carefully got on my horse and rode to camp and crawled into bed. I had not turned a cow.

The next morning we moved up and camped near a large Indian village. The Indians came around and I could see them all looking at me and talking about me.

Smiling Fox said, "Do you know what they are saying?"

I said, "No, not entirely."

He replied, "You are the greatest Medicine Man they ever saw. You got up last night and came to the herd and built a medicine fire, calmed the cattle and drove the storm away."

Nocksonna had observed all this and told them.

I was willing to accept all the credit for this but let it go at that and did not continue to practice that kind of medicine to any great extent. But they believed that I am good medicine and I sometimes think so myself as I have had some marvelous escapes in my time.

On this same trip, only a week before, we were camped at the mouth of Muddy, across the river and about four miles from where the town of Shoshoni now stands. We had about 500 head of wild steers and some dry cows and we had a large corral there. It was decided that two men would hold these cattle there for two or three days, corralling them at night. The rest of the outfit would work the Stagner Mountain.

Cal O'Neal, a halfbreed Shoshone, and myself were left there to hold the herd. We corralled them alright but the back end of the corral was weak. So we decided to bring our beds and sleep just outside the fence. If they broke the corral we would hear them. But we camped some distance from the corral down in the timber.

One evening we were late in getting supper and washing the dishes. Cal, being only a boy, had lain down on the bed and gone to sleep while I was washing the dishes. I decided not to bother him and take a chance on the corral. I laid down beside him and was soon asleep.

We were up at daylight in the morning and the cattle were gone. The boys had killed a yearling beef at the front of the corral before leaving for Stagner Mountain and the entrails lay there. In the night a bear had come up to eat these and stampeded the cattle. They had taken out the back end of the corral and where our bed would have been lay five dead cattle—trampled to death. The timbers of the corral were carried for a hundred feet. In all we lost fifteen cattle from this stampede and had about fifty crippled.

There is nothing that I know of on the range that can equal a stampede of a herd of cattle. It seems the more they run the more frightened they get and they will pile up in a gulch or go over a cliff. I think a stampede is worse than a runaway team.

So at least my good medicine helped me there.

When we got to Beaver Creek we were trimming the force down to trail to the rail head. Round Chief, another Arapaho who had been day-herding the saddle horses, came to me and soberly said, "The boys want to cut my hair. If I have my hair cut I can dance with the white girls when we get to the railroad."

I never cracked a smile. Looking at him intently for a moment I said "No, do not let them cut your hair or you will not live a year."

So they did not cut his hair. I met him just the other day and he still has long hair. Now he is a rugged man of sixty-five years.

On this same trip we were camped at Alkali Buttes and the boys found an old Indian grave in the rocks. They dug into it and got the body out, looking for Indian relics and elk teeth. They got quite a lot, although they were not of much value then. It was not unusual to see a string of forty or fifty fine teeth being worn as a string of beads.

That night the cattle were bedded near this grave. Near midnight I went up to it and placed the body back in the grave and covered it with the old pieces of buffalo robes that it had been wrapped in. I piled the rocks around and over it so the coyotes and wolves could not get at the body and gnaw the bones. I must have put a ton of rocks over him. When I had finished I lighted a match and looked at my watch. It was just midnight. A great moon was shining down on the earth and I seemed to feel the living presence of that Indian. I was not afraid and a great peace came over me. I offered up an earnest prayer to the great God of the white man and the great spirit of the Indian that my heart might ever be kind toward the Indian and that the Indian might always be my friend. I believe that prayer has been answered.

A Buffalo Hunt

I N THE FALL OF 1882 some of the Arapaho Indians told the agency clerk they were going north on a buffalo hunt. They had not got their dignity and freedom sufficiently subdued yet to ask the agent for permission to go, which was the proper thing to do.

So Sharp Nose and Friday,[1] with their following of about 200 Indians, went over the Owl Creek mountains to hunt in the Big Horn Basin. The agency heard no more of them.

The following January, upon inquiring among the Indians around the post, the agent found out the Indians had not returned and none of these Indians had drawn rations since September. Finally, the agent heard of them being down near the Big Horn Canyon. The commanding officer at Fort Washakie sent a lieutenant and ten men with an escort wagon and supplies

---

[1] Friday was only a child in 1831 when he became separated from his tribe. He was found by fur trader Thomas Fitzpatrick who took him to St. Louis. There he was placed in school and spent seven years away from his tribe. When he accompanied Fitzpatrick on one of his trading expeditions he was recognized by an Arapaho woman who claimed him as her son.

A series of brave exploits eventually earned Friday a position of leadership in his tribe and he became a principal intermediary between the Arapahos and whites. In the 1860s Friday was unique among Arapaho leaders as he continually argued in favor of avoiding military conflict with the whites. That position eventually cost him the support of many Arapaho people. During the Indian wars of 1864–1867, the U.S. government settled Friday

to go see and report. The lieutenant went and found these Indians in camp on the reservation, at the mouth of Muddy on the Big Wind River, only about sixty-five miles from the agency. The Arapahos had good luck on their hunt and secured an abundance of meat and hides, and had moved in on the reservation in November. They were camped in a splendid grove of big cottonwood trees in a big bend of the river with plenty of good, dry wood and plenty of grass for their ponies. They were living on meat and berries and did not think enough of their rations to come up and get them.

I have seen Indians take a sack of flour and empty it out on the ground and use the sack. We used to buy their coats, pants and shoes for twenty-five cents, as they would not wear them. I also remember the first Shoshone who put on a pair of pants at the agency. It was My Cat. The Shoshones had received their annuities and were laughing and talking about the pants. Some of them wanted My Cat to put his on. He did and they were too tight for him. The Indians screamed with laughter. He would twist around and look at himself, and when he would walk they would nearly die laughing. So he took them off. It was several years after that before they, of necessity, had to wear them to keep from freezing.

At first, when an Indian had a pair of pants on he kept his blanket well around him to try and hide the pants.

---

and his small band of followers near Denver. But in 1868, Friday was urged to rejoin his tribe north of the Platte River.

Sharp Nose's position in his tribe was surpassed only by Black Coal. He had worked on many occasions as a scout for the military and was accorded respect by both Arapahos and whites. When Black Coal died in 1893, Sharp Nose was accepted as the head chief of the Arapahos.

WASHAKIE GETS MAD

I THINK IT WAS IN 1885 that I was in the store at Fort Washakie when the Arapaho police brought in Edmo LeClair, a halfbreed Shoshone.[1] He was under arrest.

I never saw Washakie mad before or since, but he was surely on the war path then.

It seems Edmo had been at Fort Hall for three or four years and, coming back in the fall with his family, he had a trapper with him. They located on the lower end of the reservation, that portion occupied by the Arapahos, and built a couple of cabins.[2] In the spring they plowed up some ground and put in crops.

---

[1] Edmo (or Edmore) LeClair was not born a Shoshone, but he had ties to the Shoshone tribe which gave him undeniable acceptance. He was born to a French-Canadian father and a full-blooded Iroquois mother in upstate New York on February 3, 1847. The fate of his mother is unknown, but at a young age his father brought him west. LeClair's father later married a Shoshone–Bannock woman who bore him several children. LeClair grew up among the Indians and the remnants of the fur-trade era frontiersmen, and by 1868 he was generally accepted as a member of the tribe. In 1875 he married Phyllisete Enos, daughter of John Enos, who was of French–Flathead descent but who was also accepted as a member of the Shoshone tribe.

[2] LeClair's ranch was located on the north side of Wind River, about 14 miles west of present-day Riverton. Other sources indicate that LeClair started building his irrigation canals in 1886, so the story related here may have occurred in 1886 rather than 1885. LeClair's main canal was later extended and served as the beginning of the irrigation system that would bring water to the farming areas in the immediate vicinity of Riverton.

The Arapahos complained to the agent[3] about LeClair being down there so the agent sent a letter to LeClair telling him to report to the agency in three days. It was delivered by the Arapaho police. The three days being up and Edmo not showing up, the agent sent five Arapaho Indian police down after him. LeClair's place was fifty miles below the agency and a long day's ride. So Edmo told the police to stay all night with him and he would go with them in the morning. He fed them and then in the morning he went with them.

When they got to the hot springs about three miles below the post they met a Shoshone boy on horseback. Edmo spoke to him in Shoshone and told him to ride ahead to the store and tell Washakie to be there as he wanted to see him. The boy was greatly surprised to see a Shoshone arrested by an Arapaho and put spurs to the horse.

Washakie was there when they arrived and Edmo asked the police to stop and let him speak to Washakie for a moment. They consented, for they were very much afraid of the Shoshones. Three of the police and Edmo came in the store.

Washakie asked Edmo, "What have you been doing?"

Edmo replied, "Nothing."

Washakie replied, "They do not arrest men for nothing. What have you been doing?"

Edmo told him that he had been working like the white man said the Indian should and that he had put in a crop. The reason why he did not come in sooner was because he wanted to finish a ditch they were digging to irrigate his garden as it was badly in need of water. That was all. But the Arapahos were kicking because he was down there on their part of the reservation.

---

[3] Sanderson R. Martin or Thomas M. Jones, depending on the actual date of the incident.

Washakie rose up and said to Edmo, "Sit down."

He told the Indian police to tell the agent to come to the store.

They hesitated and Washakie, pointing his finger at them, said "Go!"

They went, and when they told the agent why they had come to his office he was very indignant. At first he refused to come and told the police to go and bring both Washakie and Edmo.

They said they would not try that as it would mean war.

So the agent had his team hitched up and came over. He came haughtily into the store and demanded the meaning of all this.

Washakie was sitting down and he motioned the agent to sit down.

The agent replied, "No, I will not sit down." He had his interpreter with him—old Norkuk.

Washakie, rising to his full height and pointing his finger at the agent, said, "Sit down."

Norkuk told the agent he had better sit down. He did, as the store was full of Shoshones by this time and a hundred of them were outside, all with their guns under their blankets.

Washakie, dropping his blanket to the floor and pointing at Edmo, addressed the agent: "You see him?"

The agent said "Yes."

"He is Shoshone, you shimbano?" ("You shimbano" means "you understand.")

The agent said "Yes."

"You see me?" Washakie asked.

"Yes," replied the agent.

Washakie continued. "I am Washakie, chief of all the Shoshones and of this reservation, you shimbano?"

The agent said "Yes."

Then Washakie turned and, pointing to the Arapahos that were present, sneeringly said, "These are beggars and dogs, and you send them to arrest a Shoshone. We should kill them all. Now, I say to Edmo this is a Shoshone reservation and he is a Shoshone and wherever his heart tells him he wants to stay on this reservation, there he may stay. You shimbano?"[4]

The agent replied that he did and, turning to the Arapaho police, said, "Don't ever arrest a Shoshone again, you shimbano?"

They did and he said they could go.

Turning to the agent, Washakie said, "You can go."

He dismissed the council and the old man was very angry for several days afterwards.

---

[4] The reservation was indeed created as the Shoshone Indian Reservation. Although the Arapahos were placed on the reservation in the 1870s, it wasn't until the 1930s that the Arapahos' legal partnership with the Shoshones was ratified by Congress.

POWDER RIVER

I N APRIL OF 1893 the *Cheyenne Leader* carried the following notice:

Roundup No. 22 will meet at Sage Creek meadows near Fort Washakie on May 10 and work up the south side of Big Wind River to the mouth of Horse Creek. Thence across Big Wind River and work down the north side to the mouth of Dry Creek. Thence up Dry Creek to its head, and thence to the head of Muddy and down to its mouth. Thence to the canyon on Big Wind River and then up Big Wind River on the north side to the mouth of Little Wind. Then the roundup will split and work up both sides of Big Wind to Merritt's crossing. Then unite and work to the head of canyon on Little Wind. Then down to junction with Big Wind. Then to mouth of Big Popo Agie and then down to its mouth. Then up Beaver to its head and then down Twin Creek to its mouth. The fall roundup to be the same, starting on September 10. Foreman is H. M. Farlow.

This roundup was composed of seven wagons and about 100 riders and about 700 head of saddle and work horses. The principal brands represented were Jules Lamoreaux (L Horsecollar and Four Jay brands), Farlow (Seventy-Four brand), Lee and Nobel (Half Circle L brand), R. H. Hall (Square and Compass brand),

John Werlen (OX brand), Colonel Jay Torrey and Captain Robert Torrey (M Bar brand), Billie O'Neal (Half Circle Cross brand), Louie and Edmo LeClair (Double Wrench brand), and Clay, Robinson and Company (71 Quarter Circle brand).

This roundup would move from six to eight miles a day. The riders would follow a leader (or three or four leaders) and would spread out like a giant fan and gather all the cattle on each side of the route taken and bring them in to the next camp. These riders would all get in to camp by noon with the cattle they had gathered. After dinner and changing horses, the men spent the afternoon working the cattle—cutting out those for holding and branding calves. Always there was a herd carried along, known as the cavvy, into which any cattle that were to be held were thrown. The cavvy was herded day and night and carried along to be disposed of as the owners saw fit. Sometimes the calves were not branded in the spring. The beef were just gathered and then the range was worked again in the fall and the calves branded then.

⧆

In the fall of 1893, the L outfit, the Four J, Horse Collar and IX outfits pooled their herds of 800 three- and four-year-old steers and dry cows to be driven to the railroad for shipment east to market. The herds were gathered at the Double Dives, on the south side of the Big Wind River, just south of where the town of Riverton now stands. When this roundup was over, the beef bearing the brands mentioned above were all put in one herd and the outfit shaped up for the long drive to the railroad.

This time the drive went to Casper. We had never shipped from Casper before and the trail was new to all the cowboys but myself.

The mess wagon was unloaded of all beds, slickers, cooking utensils and camp outfit and sent to Lander to be loaded with thirty days grub for ten men for the trip to the railroad. It was a distance of about 135 miles and we made an average of about five miles a day.

Trimmed up for the trail the outfit consisted of six cowboys: Missouri Bill, Dick Lamoreaux, Bill Lamoreaux, Arthur Roberts, Jack Rogers, and Cal O'Neal. Fred Rhody was the cook; Charles Hart was the horse wrangler; Jule Farlow was the assistant horse wrangler; and Oliver Lamoreaux was the night hawk (night horse wrangler). I was the boss.

Always before these beef herds had been trailed to some point on the Union Pacific Railroad, generally to Rawlins, but sometimes Medicine Bow or Rock Creek. Once the herd went all the way to Laramie as the feed was good. It was the boast of the foreman of a beef herd that he could put fat on his herd on the trail. And it was not unusual to lay over a few days when a good patch of feed was found. Any cowboy found driving the herd faster than a slow walk got a good calling down from the boss.

The riders were reduced to five saddle horses for the trip. We took four good work horses for the mess wagon and a couple of good work horses for extras.

When the outfit started for Casper there was seldom more than two men with the herd at one time. We just let them graze toward the next camp. The men worked in pairs and were with the cattle day and night, standing night guard in four shifts of two men each.

The night we camped on the divide between the head of Poison Creek (near where the town of Hiland now stands) and the headwaters of Dry Powder River, I told the boys we would water the herd in Powder River at about 10 o'clock the next morning. None of them had ever seen Powder River and they were all excited. In the morning when they were catching horses for the day, I called out to them to get their swimming horses as we were going to cross Powder River several times before night. Missouri Bill, who had already roped his horse, turned him loose muttering that "this damn buckskin couldn't even wade a river."

About 10 o'clock the herd reached the river and it was almost dry. The water was standing in holes and barely running from one hole to another. The herd followed down the stream for a distance of about two miles before they were watered and we crossed the river many times.

When Missouri Bill saw it he looked at it very seriously for some time and then said, "So this is Powder River."

That night in camp he told us he had heard of Powder River and now he had seen Powder River. He kept referring to Powder River nearly every day until we reached Casper.

The evening before we were going to load for shipping we bedded the cattle down near the stockyards and the boys all adjourned to the saloon for a social drink. Missouri Bill said, "Boys, come and have a drink on me. I have crossed Powder River."

They had drinks and a few more and were getting pretty sociable. When Missouri Bill ordered drinks again he said to the boys, "Have another drink on me, boys. I have swum Powder River."

This time he gave a distinct emphasis on the words "Powder River."

"Yes, sir, by damn," he added, "Powder River!"

And when the drinks were all set up he said, "Well, here's to Powder River! Let 'er buck!"

Soon he grew a little louder and was heard to say, "Powder River is comin' up! Eeeyeepe! Yes, sir, Powder River is risin'!"

Soon after, with a yip and yell, he pulled out his old six-gun and threw a few shots through the ceiling and yelled, "Powder River is up! Come and have another drink!"

Bang! Bang!

"Yeow! I'm a wolf and it's my night to howl. Powder River is out of her banks! I'm wild and wooly and full of fleas and never was curried below the knees!"

Bill was loaded for bear and that is the first time I ever heard the slogan.[1] From there it went around the world.

Bill's right name was William Shultz and I have not heard of him since. He was a good cow hand and while here he worked for the L outfit most of the time.

---

[1] Here he refers to the phrase "Powder River, let'er buck."

My Brother Needs Help

I N August of 1895 I received word that my brother Zeke had been shot through the leg at the Thermopolis hot springs. I at once saddled up a good horse and started for there.

My informer thought they might have taken him to the Embar Ranch on Owl Creek as he was working for that outfit, so I went by way of the Embar. Having eaten supper and changed horses at Stagner's on Wind River,[1] a distance of about 40 miles from Lander, I arrived at the Embar for breakfast the next morning, a distance of 100 miles.[2] They gave me a fresh horse and told me that Zeke was at Ed Enderly's house at the mouth of Owl Creek and getting along very well.

---

[1] Speed Stagner's ranch was located on Wind River in the area where Diversion Dam is now located. A natural ford there made the site a frequently used crossing place for travelers going north to the Big Horn Basin.

In the 1890s the crossing was referred to simply as Stagner's. Earlier it had been known as Merritt's Crossing. In 1877 Colonel Wesley Merritt used the crossing when he led units of the Fifth Cavalry north from Fort Washakie into the Big Horn Basin to cut off a southern escape by Chief Joseph and the Nez Perce as they made their famous race for freedom.

The crossing was used with increasing frequency in the mid-1890s as more and more settlement was taking place in the Big Horn Basin. A mail route had been established to the north. And a buckboard stage ran from Fort Washakie to Red Lodge.

[2] From Stagner's Farlow would have ridden through Mail Camp which sat at the base of the Owl Creek mountains, where the road through Blondie Pass began its climb up the face of the divide. From the top the

I arrived at Enderly's house about noon, having ridden about 130 miles without stopping, and I did it in twenty-three hours. When I stepped into the room where Zeke was lying he looked up and saw me and tears came to his eyes.

He said, "I guess I would rather see you just now than anyone else on earth."

I sat down beside him and he told me what had happened.

The roundup had camped at the hot springs and there were a few people there taking the baths. There being three or four women at the springs, the cowboys decided to have a dance and erected a crude platform out of some lumber. All were enjoying themselves immensely. Of course, when a cowboy is happy he has to whoop and yell "Powder River" and fire a few shots just to let off steam. Well, Jo Shavenaugh was doing this and throwing lead around in a reckless manner. One of the shots went squarely through Zeke's knee.[3]

It was a Colt's .45 slug so it made quite a hole. But it so happened that Dr. Schuelke from Lander was at the springs at the

---

road angled off to the northeast and finally dropped down to Owl Creek and the Embar Ranch headquarters.

Embar was the site of J.D. Woodruff's cabin—the first in the Big Horn Basin. But by 1895 Woodruff had been bought out by the Torreys—Robert and Jay. They made it one of the biggest ranches in western Wyoming and gave it the name Embar. It was a name that came from their brand: M–.

[3] Lander's *Fremont Clipper* newspaper said the "shooting was caused by the criminal recklessness of one of those crazy, drunken fools who should be caged up in a lunatic asylum or penitentiary. The fellow who did the shooting had some little altercation with Ed Dollard and struck him in the face. Not content with this, he proceeded to shoot promiscuously regardless of the risk of maiming or killing ladies or children. At the second shot, Zeke, who was standing about seven or eight steps away talking to Dollard, was seen to reel and fall. The bullet struck him on the left leg just at the knee joint, passing clear through the leg."

E.J. Farlow's brother Zeke was photographed in Lander at the turn of the century. (Photo courtesy Pioneer Museum, Lander.)

time and he took care of the wounded man, dressing the wound before any inflammation had set in. Mr. and Mrs. Enderly had been very kind in giving him room in their home. Dr. Schuelke gave me instruction as to caring for the wound and left for Lander as he was the only doctor in the country at that time and he was called from a long distance at times.[4]

---

[4] Dr. Julius Schuelke began practicing medicine in the Lander area in 1887. He provided services to people over a huge, sparsely populated area. There are many stories about his talent and skills as a physician and surgeon. And there are many other stories which talk about his drinking problems, his misuse of morphine, and extramarital affairs with women patients. In 1890 he shot and killed Lander pharmacist Isaac Sullivan in a dispute over the way Sullivan handled his prescriptions. Dr. Schuelke was convicted of the crime but served a minimal sentence. His services were needed too badly.

Dr. Schuelke began visiting the hot springs in about 1893 and named the adjacent town, Thermopolis. Later he moved from Lander to Thermopolis and became one of the towns most ardent boosters. His first wife divorced him in 1899 when he was in the Philippines serving with Torrey's Rough Riders in the Spanish American War. The grounds: adultery. Dr. Schuelke then married Lola Small, daughter of one of the nation's foremost temperance evangelists. But the reformer's precepts didn't fit with the lifestyles of either the doctor or Lola. Dr. Schuelke died in 1903 while riding the Thermopolis–Casper stage through Depass. Witnesses said he was riding quietly and slumped in his seat, suddenly dead. Many people believed that Dr. Schuelke died of an overdose of morphine.

HOLE-IN-THE-WALL-GANG

THIS LITTLE TOWN WHICH Dr. Schuelke had named Thermopolis was located four miles down the river from the famous hot springs, where the town of Thermopolis now stands. At this time a man by the name of Ben Hanson had a homestead at the mouth of Owl Creek and had platted 40 acres into town lots and had sold some. Enderly had started a little store. Higgins, Bird and McGrath had started to build a storeroom, and Neil Cunningham had built a log cabin and started a saloon. Another man (I don't remember his name) had started a blacksmith shop. Just across the river on the east side, Henry Sheard had operated a saloon for more than a year. There were not many settlers in the Big Horn Basin at this time.

I am telling you all this because at the time the hot springs area was the headquarters for the Hole-In-The-Wall gang. It was not unusual to see five or six of these men in one of the saloons at night, drinking and gambling. I was on intimate terms and very well acquainted with all of them and knew their business.

While I was there, two of them returned from a trip and stated they had cleaned up about $6,000. They were spending money very freely.

I had been there about a week when a young man by the name of William Ewing[1] drove up to the blacksmith shop to have

---

[1] Some sources give another name for this man., but contemporary newspaper accounts refer to him as J.W. Ewing.

his team shod. I was sitting outside Enderly's store and saw him drive up. I noticed he had a very nice team of gray horses and I walked over to the shop and entered into a conversation with him. He said that he had been up to the hot springs for five days just resting up and was now starting for his home in the Black Hills.

Ewing left about 5 o'clock P.M. and I bid him good luck. He said he was going to camp about five miles down the river and make about thirty miles the next day. Then, he said, he was going to push his horses for four days and try to reach home, a distance of 275 miles.

He made his short drive the second day and the next morning, after he had gone but a few miles, a masked man raised up out of a dry gulch at the side of the road and said, "Hold 'em up." The sudden sight of the outlaw frightened the team and they sprang forward and turned sharply to the left. The outlaw's gun cracked just as Ewing was turned sideways and the bullet, which was from a .45-90 Sharps rifle fired at a distance of 22 steps, struck Ewing in the right arm one inch below the elbow. The bullet broke the arm and tore a great hole in it, passed across Ewing's front tearing a great gash across his stomach which exposed his entrails, and then entered his left arm. The left arm was broken, too, so Ewing could not control the team.

By this time the team had become thoroughly frightened and had turned around and was heading back up the road in the direction from which they had come. Ewing later said he glanced over his shoulder and saw that the outlaw seemed to be having trouble with his gun. He was jerking on the lever that extracts the shell. No sooner had Ewing turned back than the gun cracked again and he felt a bullet graze his neck.

By this time the team was sending up a cloud of dust and Ewing realized he was still alive and had a chance to get away. So he began to shout at the team to urge them on.

This shooting occurred about forty miles down the Big Horn River from the present town of Thermopolis on the south side of the river. There is a big flat there that stretches for a distance of eight or nine miles and the road across this flat was very good. Had it not been for the good road, the team would have turned the buggy over. As it was, they stayed in the road and ran until they were exhausted.

In telling it later, Ewing said, "When the horses first stopped running they walked for a short distance and got their wind. Then they started off running again. But each time they would slow down a little sooner and soon they were plodding along the road on a slow walk." He would scold them and swear at them and sometimes they would trot for a short distance.

Not a house or habitation or person did he see that day until at 5 o'clock his team walked up in front of Henry Sheard's saloon, the road going right by the saloon.

He said "Whoa" to the team. An old man by the name of Knapp and a boy were sitting outside.

Ewing said, "I am hurt, will you help me out?"

They came up to him and he was a sight. He was all covered with blood. His hands were swollen as big as hams, his face was flushed and burning, and the man was all [done] in. They helped him into a little cabin nearby and the old man sent the boy across the river after me.

He came riding at a high lope to where I was sitting and said, "They want you to come over there right away; there is a man all shot to pieces."

At once I thought the outlaws had had a row among themselves.

Taking some bandages and medicine the doctor had left for me, I went over and there lay the young man I had seen at the blacksmith shop two days before. When I looked at him I thought, "He is a dead man, sure."

I had some experience in treating wounds and there being no one else there to do it, I rolled up my sleeves and started in on him, stripping the bloody clothes off him. I found the bullet—a big lump on the outside of the left elbow. Taking a razor of Henry Sheard's, I took just one stroke and I had the bullet out. Ewing fainted away at this, but we sprinkled cold water in his face and bathed his head for a short time and he came out of it alright.

I was about two hours bandaging and washing his wounds. After I had him fixed up the best I could I sat down beside his bed and asked him if he had any idea who fired the shots.

He said, "Yes, I knew him. I recognized him by his clothes, his build and his voice. I met him up at the springs and he tried to get me into a game of cards with him."

We found $165 in cash in his clothes and I gave it to a woman by the name of Mrs. Stead to keep for him.

Now, to show you the spirit of these outlaws here.

The man wanted a doctor and Schuelke at Lander was the nearest. Dusty Jim, a very common sort of a chap who was one of the gang said, "I will go for a doctor."

Mounting his horse he started at about 8 o'clock and the next day was in Lander, a distance of 100 miles, on one horse. I had ridden it by way of Embar, 130 miles, on three horses, and thought I had done wonders.

The next day he started back with Schuelke in a buggy, leading the horse behind.

On the third day we had a doctor who, after examining Ewing, said "Hell, Farlow, he is doing alright." So Dr. Schuelke gave some instructions, dressed the wounds once, returned to Lander, and charged the man $125.

In reply to my question as to who shot him, Ewing said it was Slick Nard, a desperado who had been hanging around there for a couple of weeks. I was not sure if he was one of the gang or not.[2]

About this time Slick Nard came riding up to the saloon from the opposite direction. Soon Henry Sheard came to me and said, "Ed, I believe I have the man that did this job."

I asked him who and he named Slick. I told him that was the man Ewing named.

Sheard said "What shall we do?"

I said, "Keep still until morning and we will grab him."

Johnson County had just been organized and Charley Anderson, a rancher about a mile down the creek, had been appointed a Justice of the Peace.[3] So the next morning we got a warrant for Slick Nard, charging him with felonious assault. Henry Sheard and another husky young fellow there who was not in sympathy with the gang were deputized to arrest him. I told them not to take a chance, "If he makes a move, begin shooting."

Slick had gone up to the springs (where the present city of Thermopolis stands) while we were getting the papers so it was necessary for them to go up there after him, a distance of about four miles. Arriving there they discovered Slick's horse tied near a tent that was open at both ends. Riding up quietly,

---

[2] Albert "Slick" Nard was best known as a member of a group of thieves that operated in the Big Horn Basin. Led by Jack Bliss, they operated out of a base in the Owl Creek Mountains and stole from the larger cattle and horse herds in the basin.

[3] Thermopolis was a part of Fremont County and Charley Anderson would have served as a Fremont County Justice of the Peace. But the crime was committed in Johnson County and so Johnson County would have had jurisdiction in the crime.

they dismounted and one of them arrived at each end of the tent at the same time with their guns in their hands.

They told Slick to stick them up, which he did, at the same time asking, "What the hell is the matter with you fellows?"

When they told him they wanted him for the shooting of Ewing he replied with a confident air, "If that's all you want, I can explain that all right as I was at the Birdseye Ranch on the other side of the mountains and stayed all night with Dave Hanks."[4]

They brought Nard down to Sheard's saloon. As we had no place to hold him, Sheldon, the other deputy, herded him.

When I came over from the other side that evening to dress Ewing's wounds I saw the men around the saloon with their guns on their hips. Slick was walking around and talking with them. Sheldon was watching him. I told Sheard that in an unguarded moment Slick would grab a gun and kill the guard and go.

I went back across the river and got a trace chain from a set of chain harness and sent it over with a padlock. They knocked the chinking out between the logs in a little cabin there and, the chain having a ring in one end, they looped it around the log in the cabin. It took just three links to reach around Slick's ankle. They snapped the padlock in and had him solid.

When he saw what they were going to do he begged of them to not chain him up and promised to obey and follow them like a "yaller dog," as he put it. But they locked him up just the same. Then he cursed them to everything he could think of, and he knew all the words.

I had been Justice of the Peace and U.S. Commissioner at Lander for some time and had a number of cases before me.

---

[4] Birdseye Ranch was located in the foothills below Birdseye Peak and Copper Mountain, on the Wind River Valley side of the divide.

And I will say here that I also had a number of Indians brought before me for offenses of various kinds. So, with my experience in the Justice Court, I acted as adviser for the court and also for Slick. I told Slick he would be allowed to subpoena any witness he wanted to testify on his behalf. If he wanted Dave Hanks brought over, an officer would go after him.

Now the Birdseye Ranch he named was south of the scene of the shooting about sixty miles. It would have been impossible for him to have been at the shooting that morning if he had been at the Birdseye Ranch all night and took breakfast with Old Dry (that was the nickname for Dave Hanks). But when we offered to send for Hanks, Nard said it would be of no use as Hanks was going to go to Lander that day and would be gone for a week. And when he refused to send for Hanks we knew he had not been there.

The next day three men went down to the scene of the shooting. There had been no one else along that way and no wind so the tracks were as plain as when they were first made. The men found where the bandit had his horse tied to a tree, out of sight. From the tracks, it looked as if he had waited for his victim all night. He had led his horse down to the Big Horn River to water. The water level was falling so the bandit's tracks and the horse's tracks were as plain in the wet sand as it was possible for tracks to be. They could count the tacks in the soles of his boots. The horse had lost a shoe and had a badly broken hoof. It was twenty-two steps from where they picked up the shells of the gun to where Ewing's team had turned out of the road and made the short turn around. The tracks showed the team was running at good speed when it came into the road after turning around. The shells lying around had been hit by a firing pin that was square and homemade.

Slick had borrowed Henry Sheard's Sharps rifle, a .45-90. Henry had earlier made a firing pin for it out of the end of a nail. Henry also loaded his own shells and made his own bullets. He had worked his bullet molds over and was using a two-ring bullet. All the regular Sharps ammunition used a three-ring bullet. The bullet I cut out of Ewing's arm was a two-ring bullet.

A date three days after the shooting was set for the hearing. Anderson and I thought the state had sufficient evidence to hold Nard for trial. It was a nice warm day in August and the case was called in Justice Anderson's court for 2 P.M. In this case the court was brought to the defendant as Anderson, the two deputies and myself went to the cabin where Slick was chained. We brought him out in front of Sheard's saloon and the complaint was read to him very solemnly by the court. Again he pleaded "Not guilty."

All of this seemed to Anderson, Sheard and myself the greatest farce that had ever been enacted, for there was at that time in that immediate vicinity the most desperate gang of outlaws the West had ever known. There was Butch Cassidy, Al Hainer, Bob McCoy, Jakey Snyder, Dusty Jim, Mike Brown, Tom Horn, Jim McCloud, Kise Eads and one or two lesser lights.[5] I knew all these men and knew what their business was. And I was well acquainted with and on easy and friendly terms with all of them. Here were half a dozen of us law abiding citizens trying to enforce the law in the midst of this gang. They were in the majority and more than once I asked Anderson, "How long will

---

[5] Farlow's inclusion of Tom Horn on this list is curious. No other sources suggest that Horn was ever a part of the Hole-In-The-Wall gang. In fact, Horn was best known for his work for large cattle interests to discourage rustling.

The shooting of Ewing apparently caused Fremont County authorities to action against lawless element in the region. The *Fremont Clipper* "heartily and earnestly applauded…the determination of the officers of Fremont County to bring the thieves to justice…. Deputy Sheriff [Jim] Baldwin is still on the hunt and it is hoped he will make a good record." But Baldwin's efforts were less than successful. Two weeks later the *Clipper* reported that

they let this thing go on." I fully expected at any time some of them would pull their guns and walk up to us or our deputy and say, "Turn him loose." And it would have been done.

Slick evidently had some previous experience in court for he seemed well informed. He waived examination and said he believed we had sufficient evidence to hold him. He was very meek and asked the Honorable Court to fix his appearance bond as light as possible. He made no showing at this time but said he could easily clear himself in the District Court which was to be held in Buffalo in November.

Anderson asked me what I thought was reasonable and I replied, "Ewing is liable to die at any time and this man will then be charged with murder and no bond is allowed. I suggest you hold this man without bond."

He did and Slick gave me such a look I shall never forget.

The court then instructed the two deputies to get ready to start for Buffalo with their prisoner early in the morning.

Everything was prepared the evening before. About 9 o'clock I rode over to Sheard's saloon to see if they were alright. Sheard had gone to the corral in back of the saloon some little distance and I went there. I told him to get his horses ready and get down the road a few hundred yards. Sheldon would bring Slick over to the saloon to get a drink and give him a chance to say good-bye to the rest of them. Afterwards, instead of going back to the cabin, they would walk right by the cabin in the dark and come on down to where Sheard was waiting. They were to mount and go immediately in an effort to elude the gang. We thought surely they would not let us take him away.

"Baldwin returned from his northern trip…after an absence of nearly three weeks spent in the useless endeavor to capture some noted criminals. The plan of the expedition was interfered with by dispatches published in Omaha, which gave an outline of his business…"

At the hearing there were six or eight of these outlaws sitting around. Some of them were on their horses, all of them had guns on. They never said a word except, perhaps, when they were joking about something. To say we felt small is putting it mild.

On the west side of the river lived Ed Enderly and his wife, Tom Bird and his wife, Mrs. Stead and her daughter (who ran a little eating house), Neil Cunningham (who ran a saloon), Ben Hanson (who owned the town), the blacksmith, Ed Sheldon, and Henry Sheard. One or two others lived on the east side. My brother Zeke was in Enderly's house with a broken leg and Ewing was in a cabin on the east side with both arms broken and a bad wound in the stomach. This was the population as near as I can recall it at this time, aside from the gang.

In the morning there was a little excitement when I came over to dress Ewing's wounds. Slick and the deputies were gone and no one knew just how. Several of the boys were at the saloon talking about it. When I rode up they told me Slick had gone.

I said, "Yes, I know it. He should be on the top of Ten Sleep Mountain now on his way to Buffalo."

Mike Brown spoke up and asked what was the big idea.

I told him straight. "We did not know how soon you fellows would say 'turn him loose.'"

Mike replied, "Turn that son of a bitch loose? If you had said the word we would have helped you hang him. I want you to know this, Farlow. We may rob a bank, or hold up a stage or a railroad pay car now and then, but we are not killing working men for their money. We are not that damn low yet."

We found that Slick was playing a lone hand in this and did not let anyone know his plans. If he had succeeded in killing his man and had, perhaps, thrown the body in the river, no one would have ever known.

I stayed there about two weeks after this and, having sent to Lander for my team and buggy, took Zeke home to Lander.

Slick Nard was tried before Judge Metz at Buffalo and found guilty. The judge, in sentencing him, said "The legislature of this state has been too lenient for offenses of this kind; they have fixed the extreme penalty at fourteen years. I will sentence you to fourteen years imprisonment and, you scoundrel, I am sorry I cannot give you more."

Ewing got well, but I never saw him again.

WILCOX TRAIN ROBBERY

I N THE SUMMER OF 1897 there was a holdup and train robbery of the Union Pacific train on the Laramie Plains at a little station called Wilcox. It was reported that the robbers got $100,000. There were six robbers.[1]

The gang split and three of them were trailed north. They were closely pressed by Sheriff Joe Hazen of Converse County in the badlands at the head of the Dry Powder River. The robbers turned on Hazen and his posse and a fight ensued. Joe Hazen was killed.[2] The robbers were cornered in the rough washouts and had to abandon their horses to get away.

Butch Cassidy was one of these and after the fight they separated. They were headed for their rendezvous at the mouth of

---

[1] The Wilcox train robbery took place on June 2, 1899. There are conflicting stories as to the amount of money stolen however it's likely that they got about $34,000 in cash and several thousand dollars in national bank notes.

[2] This shootout took place on June 5 in the rocky country along Dugout Creek, about 30 miles north of Casper. The outlaws were successful in pinning down the eleven-man posse and shot two of the posse's horses. Sheriff Joe Hazen and a Union Pacific Railroad detective by the name of Wheeler worked their way through the rocks until suddenly, about 75 yards away, the outlaws rose and fired on them. Hazen was shot in the stomach but Wheeler escaped injury. Hazen couldn't be moved until a spring wagon was brought in, and the rough country made it impossible to get him to medical help quickly. He died shortly after being brought back to Douglas.

Owl Creek on the Big Horn. Knowing that the whole country would be aroused by the killing of the sheriff—he was a great favorite and a mighty fine man—they decided wisely that it would not be safe for them, even in that area.

Such was the case, for Jeff Carr[3] from Cheyenne gathered a posse of about 30 good men and went into the stronghold of these outlaws. He found nothing.

Securing a horse at a sheep ranch, Cassidy rode into Lander and was concealed for two days in the back room of Lannigan's saloon. He and Joe Lannigan were great friends and Joe had a stable just back of the saloon in which he always kept a good saddle horse. After resting for two days Cassidy left Lander in the night and rode Joe's horse, Old Whiskey, out to another friend who lived on the reservation where he rested for two weeks. This man's name was Emery Burnaugh and he told me that Butch had about $40,000. After his stay at Burnaugh's, Cassidy left the country and said he was going to go straight down to South America.[4]

---

[3] T. Jeff Carr was only one of the many men who got involved in the search for the Wilcox robbers. Even Tom Horn was involved. Horn claimed to have killed two of the robbers in the mountains forty miles west of Jackson Hole and may have received a reward from Union Pacific. The well-known stock detective Joe LeFors took a posse into the Thermopolis country and came up empty-handed. He later intimated that the reason for his failure was that former Fremont County Sheriff Arthur Sparhawk purposely led them off on a wild goose chase through the Owl Creek mountains when they were within two hours of catching up with the gang.

[4] Emery and Alice Burnaugh had known Butch Cassidy for years and they considered him a good friend. A Burnaugh family story relates that Cassidy was with a group of men on this occasion and that they camped under a sandstone outcropping on Muddy Creek, several hundred yards from Burnaughs' road ranch. An unmarked grave adjacent to the Burnaugh family cemetery on the bluff above the outlaws' campsite is supposed to be that of one of the Wilcox robbers who had been wounded in the chase and

I used to know George Cassidy quite well. The first time I saw him, he and Al Hainer came into Lander to spend the winter.[5] They had evidently just made a good haul for they seemed to have plenty of money and spent it freely. Neither of them were much for drinking but they were great for gambling.

I was running the dances in Lander that winter and my wife taught Cassidy to waltz. One night, after coming home from a dance, she remarked to me that Cassidy always had a gun under his coat. She could feel it when dancing with him. It was customary for most of the men to wear guns in those days but they usually took off their guns and spurs and left them behind the bar while dancing.

❖

I gave dances and called for dances and managed dances in Lander for thirty-five years. In that time I have had several desperate characters to deal with — both male and female — and I have never had a dance broken up or had much of a scene in the ballroom. I have had to ask several persons out, and it has not been a pleasant task in several cases. As a rule the women are the worst as I can talk to a man as a man and I have used some very clever diplomacy in a few cases. I found that even with the worst drunk, or the most desperate bad man, an appeal to his manhood

---

who died shortly after arriving at the Burnaugh ranch.

Cassidy did not, however, leave for South America at this time. Reliable documentation indicates that his trip to South America did not occur until 1902.

[5] Al Hainer was with Butch Cassidy in 1889 when he first came into the Wind River Country. Together they established a horse ranch on Horse Creek in the Dubois area. Hainer was arrested with Cassidy in 1892 and charged with stealing horses. When the case was finally tried in 1893, Cassidy was found guilty while Hainer was acquitted. There are indications that Hainer may have double-crossed Cassidy and struck a deal with the prosecutors or witnesses for the prosecution.

was the most effective way to handle him. Only once or twice was it necessary to use force.

I won a signal victory one night over a desperate gang of toughs who were determined to break up the dance an any cost. Not that they had anything against me, but there were two factions and one of them seemed to have the floor. The others were about to begin action when I got wind of what was going on. Calling John Seminole, Bob Jackson and Cotton Hook Jackson to one side (these were the ring leaders of the gang), I took them in the saloon and we all had a drink. I told them confidentially that there was a gang of tough boys who were going to break up the dance and scare the women half to death. I intimated that it was a small group of soldiers from Fort Washakie but did not say as much. I asked the ring leaders if I could count on them to stand by me if the toughs started anything. They all grasped me by the hand and said I could. I told them to hang around and dance whenever they felt like it, but be ready for a signal from me.

We had another drink. They felt very important to be called on to quell a disturbance.

Now and then they would ask me how much longer I thought it would be and we would have another drink. Soon I had Big Jackson laid out, and then Seminole followed. I gave them another drink and the battle was won. Whiskey won it for me.

※

This Hole-In-The-Wall gang continued to be strong in the Big Horn Basin until 1905. For two or three years before this time they had been doing a lot of cattle stealing and it was impossible for the stockmen in that country to get any evidence to convict them. One of their number, Mike Brown, had started a butcher shop in Thermopolis and was doing a good business. Other members of the gang were stealing the beef for him. The cattlemen were getting desperate and, you know, desperate diseases require desperate remedies.

One evening in August, Bob McCoy bought some steak for supper and started home. McCoy was associated with the gang and he lived across the river and up about a mile. He never got home. The next day, during a search, they found him in the river, just above the ford. He had been shot. A nosebag was around his neck. It was filled with rocks. And one ear was cut off.

This struck terror to the hearts of the rest of the gang for they knew the man that did this would collect a goodly sum as a bounty from the cattlemen. They had no idea from whence it came. Kize Eads, Jim McCloud, Dusty Jim, Al Hainer and some of the lesser lights got up and "quit the country," as the saying is, right now.

Eads said, "They don't have to tell me twice, I am going."

Jakey Snyder stayed around town—afraid to move. Mike Brown stayed too. Two years later Bill George killed Jakey Snyder—said he was monkeyin' around with his wife. A year later Mike Brown's wife killed him. The story was that he came home drunk and was going to beat her up. The wise ones winked one eye and said there was a man behind the gun.

This ended the Hole-In-The-Wall gang except for Tom O'Day. And he stayed around and behaved himself.[6]

---

[6] Tom O'Day's most significant outlaw escapade came in 1897 when he was arrested with Walt Punteney in connection with the holdup of a bank at Belle Fourche, South Dakota. But testimony by Mike Brown and Bob McCoy apparently convinced the jury that O'Day and Punteney had taken dinner one night before the Belle Fourche robbery at Brown's ranch near Thermopolis.

A prominent Big Horn Basin rancher once said, "Tom ain't a bad fellow when you get to know him. He's just a big, good-natured kid that thinks he is having a good time."

O'Day's good times often involved horses. He frequently raced horses on the Cheever's Flat area on No Wood River. At a restaurant in the area, O'Day was once attacked by an "armed enemy." As this "enemy" approached O'Day with revolver blazing, O'Day stood and threw pieces of chinaware from his table. The gunman's weapon ran out of shells before O'Day could be hit. And the attacker ended up on the sidewalk, crowned with a soup plate.

And contrary to Farlow's testimony, O'Day didn't stay completely clean. In 1904 he began a four-and-a-half-year term in the Wyoming Penitentiary for horse stealing. When he was released he returned to the Lost Cabin area where he lived in a dugout for a number of years. He died in 1930 at Fort Pierre, South Dakota when a runaway team overturned a wagon in which he was riding.

CATTLE KATE

I N 1889 THERE WAS A woman living in a cabin on the Sweetwater, just below Devil's Gate. She had a bootlegging joint and was quite a favorite with the outlaws in that vicinity.

They called her Cattle Kate and she had quite a bunch of cattle. Her herd seemed to be growing very fast and the cattlemen there were getting tired of it. She had a boy who was about twelve years old. An old fellow named Jim Averill [Averell] was choring around the place. Averill was a harmless old man.[1]

One morning they found Jim Averill and Cattle Kate hanging from a tree not far from the cabin and the cattlemen lost no more calves for several years after that.[2]

---

[1] Cattle Kate's real name was Ella Watson but she was sometimes referred to as Kate Maxwell. She had a cabin and corrals on the Sweetwater where some thought she worked as a prostitute. Jim Averell ran a saloon and store about a mile from Watson's cabin. Although he is frequently described as sickly, he was only 44 years old and was certainly more significant than "a harmless old man." Averell had gained a reputation as a smart and feisty opponent of some of the big ranchers in the area. His sharply-worded letters to Wyoming newspapers accusing those ranchers of fraudulent acquisitions of huge tracts of grazing lands may have been of greater concern to the ranchers than Watson's suspicious acquisition of a few cattle.

The boy who was at Watson's cabin is not believed to have been her son. His name was Gene Crowder.

[2] A coroner's inquest named several Sweetwater areas ranchers as being a part of the group of men which hanged Watson and Averell. The group included A.J. Bothwell, Tom Sun, John Durbin, R.M. Galbraith, Bob Connor, M. Ernest McLean and an unknown man. That unknown man was

I must tell you of an incident that happened a few years before this that had to do with Cattle Kate.

I was sent as a rep to the Sweetwater roundup in '84, I think it was, and we were camped just above Devil's Gate. The outfit was composed of eight wagons, as I remember, and about one-hundred men. Dinner was over and we had caught and saddled fresh horses and were all ready to go out and work the cattle that had been brought in on the morning drive. I was standing, ready to mount my horse, when I saw three men talking in low tones about fifteen feet from me. One of them had a piece of paper in his hand and I heard him say, "You had better come along."

It was the sheriff of Carbon County and his deputy. They were talking to Bill Young, an outlaw.

Bill said, "I don't know if I want to go or not."

The deputy had a gun in his hand and said, "We will take you."

Just then, on my right and not more than ten feet away, a voice spoke up and said, "I guess, by God, he don't go."

Looking around I saw about a dozen guns leveled on the officers. It was Nate Young, a brother of Bill's, who had spoken.

He continued, "Now you get on your horses and ride, and don't look back."

And they went.

A year later, when the roundup came up Sweetwater, Bill Young stopped to visit Kate. He was watchful and got away alright. But he came back from the roundup the next day and spent the night there at Kate's. In the morning, when he came

---

believed to have been George B. Henderson. A Rawlins grand jury later refused to indict the members of the group. Three potential witnesses had disappeared and another had died from what a doctor claimed was Bright's disease.

out, he walked into the guns of the sheriff of Carbon County. They took him to Rawlins.

As soon as they were gone, Kate sent her boy on a good horse to tell the boys at the roundup. I saw him ride into camp. Riding up to Nate Young and Bill Foster he said, "They have got Bill."

They saddled up good, fresh horses and, accompanied by Cheeko and Jim Brown (two more outlaws), made a straight run for Rawlins, about sixty miles away.

Bill Foster told me they got to the Paint Mines, which is about a mile out from Rawlins, where they could plainly see the town, just in time to see an eastbound passenger train pull out. They knew that Bill was on it. He was wanted in Texas for killing a man. It was three days before they got back to the roundup.

There were three of these Young brothers—Nate, Bill and Clabe—who drifted into Montana from here. Nate got killed resisting arrest. Clabe, I am told, died in prison. I saw a man the other day who said Bill was still living in a little cabin in Montana under the name of Jones. This man said he stopped overnight and camped near Bill and had quite a visit with him. When he told Bill that he knew Ed Farlow and was going to Lander and would see him, Bill told him who he was and said to tell Ed hello for him.

These fellows were good range hands and good fellows to work with. Most of them had fled from some other state for some crime or other and many of them were under assumed names. I worked with them, ate with them and slept with them. I knew what they were but I did not make their business my business. They never bothered me and would talk quite freely to me at times of the scrapes they had been in and—sometimes— of the jobs they had pulled off.

THE CUSTER FIGHT

I HAVE MET MANY INDIANS who were in the Custer Battle and have asked them to tell me just what happened. I have been told by many of them about the fight as they saw it. I am going to give it to you from the Indian standpoint, for they were there and lived to tell it.

When I first became acquainted with the Lamoreaux family I took a great liking to one of the boys. William Lamoreaux was six years younger than myself. He was half Sioux and half French and his Indian name was Smiling Fox—so named because he was always smiling. He took a great liking to me and we were pals from that time on. We were always together when it was possible.

One night Smiling Fox and I were stopping in the tepee of an old Arapaho Indian who was camped at the mouth of Beaver. The Indian was called Plenty Bear. Now Plenty Bear was what we would call a historian; that is, he had been told much of the history of his people by the older Indians. That is the only history they ever had that I know of. They do not have these historians now as they have learned to write these things down. But before the days of the white man they would pick out a bright youth and make him a depository of the traditions of the tribe. When I first came among them, they would say this man or that knows the history as he has been told this by the old Indians and it is his place to remember and tell it to some younger one.

After supper was over we were sitting quietly, smoking. Smiling Fox spoke to me in the sign language and said, "Plenty Bear was in the Custer fight."

Turning to him, I asked him in the sign language if he was at the fight.

Looking at me intently for a moment he asked me in the sign language, "Why do you ask?"

I replied in the same way. "The half Sioux has told me you were."

He studied me for a moment and, looking up, said "You are my friend, I will tell you. I was."

I then asked him why he had not told me sooner as this was twenty years after the battle.

He replied that he was afraid the big white chief at Washington would hear of it and put him in jail. He had heard that a lot of the Sioux had been put in jail for killing the soldiers.

He said, "Two snows before that fight I put my thumb on a piece of paper (meaning he had signed a peace treaty) to be a good Indian and not fight the white man any more."

He knew the Sioux were going to have a fight with the soldiers and that the Sioux were good fighters. The Sioux were great friends of the Arapahos so about twenty-five of the young Arapahos had gone to Sitting Bull's camp on the Greasy Grass. They had quietly left the Arapahos who were down on the Platte around Fort Robinson at that time. They joined the Sioux just to be in one more good fight against the white man.

Gall told him that it did not take the medicine of Sitting Bull to tell them they were going to have a fight with the soldiers. They all knew the soldiers were out hunting for them and when they found them they would have a fight. The Sioux did not intend to go to the reservation as the white chief wanted them to.

I told Plenty Bear that they would not bother him as it was only the leaders of the Sioux who were punished, and that it was all over now.

Plenty Bear then began to talk.

He told me that he had a very clear conception of what took place. He said the twenty-five Arapahos joined the Cheyennes under Crazy Horse and Two Moons on the head of Powder River. General Crook got after them and for twenty days they fled before the white soldiers.

Five days before the Custer fight they had a fight with Crook's scouts and some of his soldiers. The Indians were getting short of meat and ammunition, and their horses were getting down and out. So after that fight with the scouts they hurried up and got over to the Greasy Grass as they knew there were lots of buffalo in there and they expected to find a lot of Sioux camped there. They knew Sitting Bull and his followers were there and were going to fight the soldiers when they came.

The next day, when the soldiers appeared, they thought it was Crook's army that had hurried up after them. But they were glad when they found so many Sioux, along with Gall, the great war chief of the Hunkpapas, and all of his warriors. He knew the soldiers could not whip them.

Now I will quote you Mrs. Spotted Horn Bull, wife of the young chief by that name, who told me in very good English of the fight. She was camped at about the center of the village which was up and down the river for three miles.

She said, "I stood outside of my tepee and saw the battle. The scouts brought in the word that the soldiers were coming and the women had their packs all ready for a hurried move if the battle went against them. At a council meeting, after the Cheyennes had come into camp and reported their fight with the soldiers, it was decided they would stand and fight but would not go out after the soldiers if they would not bother them. Reno surprised them when he fired into the upper end of the village. Gall and his men swept through the village like the wind going to repulse Reno which he did very soon. Reno's men crossed the river and got off their horses quick on the hill and laid down and could shoot easily at the Indians, who did not try to get them while they could not see them. About this time Custer's army came into sight and Gall took his men and went to meet him. There were very few Indians firing at Reno at this time. The soldiers came to within a half-mile of the river and stopped (here she made the sign as if they were looking through field glasses) and stood there for quite awhile.

"Gall and the Hunkpapa warriors, 1,000 strong, were directly in front of the soldiers. Gall was sending Indians to the right and to the left, up the ravines, telling them to keep out of sight.

"The Indian forces included the Minneconjous (under Lame Deer), Hump, the Oglalas (under Big Road), Two Moons and Crazy Horse (leading the Cheyennes), and Gall, Crow King, John Grass, Black Moon and Spotted Horn Bull (leading the Hunkpapas). The Hunkpapas were the fighting Indians of the entire Sioux nation. The name Hunkpapas means "defenders of the camp" or "camped on the outside." You might be born of another tribe and become a Hunkpapa by moving your tepee out in the direction from whence the danger might come, and by declaring yourself ready to fight and die, if necessary, to protect the village.

"The Sanarcs and Minneconjous went up the draws on one side, the Cheyennes and Oglalas on the other. Gall with his warriors met them. Finally they heard the bugle and the soldiers came marching down toward the river. Gall and his men went across and most them were out of sight under a little rise or hill. The soldiers fired the first shots and hit a young Sioux in the rear of Gall's men and he fell off his horse in the river."

Mrs. Spotted Horn Bull told me the name of this Indian but I have forgotten it.

"He came back to the camp and was badly wounded and the women were very much excited. About this time Gall and his men were just rising the hill and met the soldiers. They rode very slowly, chanting their war song, advancing."

Now a great many people think a war song should be a fierce and terrible thing, but such is not the case. It is a low chant, a continual prayer to the Great Spirit to give them strength and power to overcome their enemies and to protect them. It is also intended to tell the Great Spirit "You see my heart. I have done no wrong. You see my hands, they have done no wrong. Be with us and help us."

Mrs. Spotted Horn Bull continued: "After the first shock of battle the troops immediately retreated and if they had continued to go they could have gotten away. But they did not. And after gaining higher ground they stopped. The white men were fools. They did not know how to fight. They sat erect on their horses and were targets for the Indians. The Indians in that day would lie flat on the side of their ponies and expose nothing but an arm and leg to the fire of the enemy. When they saw the Indians coming in sight behind and at the sides of the soldiers, they knew that none would escape."

Mrs. Spotted Horn Bull was glad of this because her brother White Eye Brows and her husband were in the fight. The fight did not last long, about thirty minutes, as she described it.

The first they knew in the village of the result was when a young Indian, a brother of Running Antelope, came riding down the hill and across the river at full speed on a big, gray soldier's horse, waving a bloody scalp and shouting, "We have killed them all. We have killed them all." He ran here and there through the village, drunk with victory.

Then the women and children flocked to the battleground. Most of the mutilating was done by the women and boys. Whenever a woman or boy had a friend or loved one killed or wounded in a fight, they immediately fell on the first body they found and beat and hacked and took their revenge out on it. The warriors took the clothes, guns, horses, scalps and other trophies of war, but left the naked bodies lay.

There was great rejoicing in the village that night for never had they won so great a victory with so little loss. As near as Mrs. Spotted Horn Bull could tell, the soldiers had killed sixty-five Indians and wounded many more. Sitting Bull was not in the fight.

Sitting Bull, contrary to the generally accepted tradition, was not a warrior. You would describe him today as a religious politician. He was a medicine man, an inveterate hater of the white man. He had been making medicine in the camp for a month and he was highly rated as a medicine man. He had been dancing, fasting, and praying. They had religious dances and he had invoked the aid of the Great Spirit to the arms of the Sioux. He told them they were going to have a great battle with the white man and would gain a great victory. He had inspired confidence in the Indians. Also, their increasing numbers inspired confidence. And the arrival of Crazy Horse and Two Moons with about 1,000 of the fighting Cheyennes just the day before gave them greater confidence. They had been saving their ammunition to fight the white man and had been killing buffalo with bows and arrows and spears.

Plenty Bear said that after it was all over—the next morning—the women came to a realization of what it all meant and their scouts brought in the news that the walking soldiers were coming. They were very much afraid. Tears came to their eyes and they said the soldiers would come and kill all of them because they had killed these men. They hurried and packed up and pulled out. The men threatened Reno's position on the hills so he would not attack them and by noon all the Indians were gone—except the warriors that were watching Reno.

Plenty Bear says they had lots of baggage and they did not have enough ponies to carry everything. So, showing the Indian characteristics, many of the women had to walk. He said there was one nice young Sioux girl who had just been married and her husband was killed in the fight. She got the body and would not bury it. She kept it and loaded it on a travois and carried it for five days and cried over it at night. The body got to smelling bad and one night, after dark, some of the women got her to go a little way from the body. The men took it into the darkness and buried it. She hunted for it and would not go on the next morning. She stayed behind but came into camp later.

One woman walked with two children. She carried her baby on her back but the other—about six years old—walked beside her. When the child would get tired and lie down she would get a stick and whip it and make it get up and go. The child's moccasins were worn through and the bottoms of his feet were bleeding.

It would be midnight sometimes before all of them were in camp. Many of the other tribes dropped out in small bunches and went in different directions. Some of the Arapahos had already gone and the rest of the Arapahos left them before they got into Canada. They came back to their tribes and pretended to know nothing of the fight.

BUFFALO HUNT

I SAW OLD RUNNING Antelope, a Sioux and one of the chiefs in the Custer fight, in 1923 here on the Wind River Reservation. He and another Sioux had come up here from Standing Rock Reservation and I was talking to him of a great buffalo hunt the Sioux had in 1882.

He was a leader of the hunt and became greatly interested when I told him I was there. He said that he knew there were some white men there but not many. The agent McLaughlin[1] and his son were there along with some of the white employees from the agency (five teamsters with supplies) and two other cowboys.

About the first of June, 1882 Smiling Fox and myself were with the Powder River roundup and were camped not far from where the town of Salt Creek now is. We saw signs of oil at that time and could have taken up a section of land there but we did not know its value.

There came into camp one evening two young Sioux Indians with tired horses and asked to stay all night. We stopped them at once and they were glad to find a friend. We learned that they were going to the Standing Rock Reservation and that the Sioux were going to have a great buffalo hunt right now and

---

[1] This is James McLaughlin, who later had extensive contact with the Indians of the Wind River Indian Reservation.

they were hurrying to get there. They were already late and expected to meet them as they were coming west to hunt. By morning, Smiling Fox and I had decided to take in that buffalo hunt. The other boys were turning back from there to go to Wind River with what cattle they found (which was not many). So we packed our beds on a horse and with two good saddle horses each and two pack horses we started with the two Indians for the buffalo hunt.

In five days we arrived, just in time to see the Indians organize the hunt. We met them about sixty miles off the agency. There were about 3,000 of them. They had about forty wagons and over 1,000 ponies packed and dragging travois and tepee poles. They traveled in two broad columns, about a hundred yards apart. They moved very slowly as hundreds of them were walking.

The morning after we got there the men adjourned to the plain just west of the camp and seated themselves in a semi-circle. At the left of this half-moon sat the men of rank. Out about ten feet sat Running Antelope, the chief of the hunt. Eight young men were chosen for scouts who were to go ahead and see what was to be found and report. They were to be sworn in. They had found a stone about a foot high and this was painted by the medicine man and used for an altar. The young men were squatted on the ground opposite the leader and he addressed them, telling them they had been selected from the entire village because of their honesty and ability. They were to go forward to work diligently and truthfully report all they had found. They were to look for game, for wood and water, for camping and for grass for the ponies. The leader then filled the sacred pipe and, taking a coal from the medicine fire that had to be kept burning during the ceremony, he lighted it. Taking a couple of long whiffs to see that it was well lighted, he passed it to the first scout. He took a long draw and passed it to the next, and so on to the last.

E.J. Farlow was photographed in the 1930s by a National Park Service photographer in connection with a historical project. (Photo courtesy of Pioneer Museum, Lander.)

When this was done and the pipe handed back to Running Antelope, he knocked out the fire and ashes from the pipe and the ceremony was over.

Immediately there was wild confusion. Indians to the number of 100 mounted to escort the scouts on their way. This was all a part of the medicine and ceremony that had to be followed in order to assure the success of the hunt. The riders escorted the scouts for a distance of about a mile and while they were gone the greater number of the Indians remained seated in this semi-circle with its horns pointing to the west. The medicine man got up and stuck three green bushes, one at each end and one near the center of this semi-circle, about twenty feet in front of the sitting Indians. At a given signal, all the escorts who were with the scouts turned and raced back to see who could be the first to ride down these bushes. If only one of the bushes was knocked down, the hunt would be poor. If two were knocked down it would be fair, and if by chance all three were rode down, the hunt would be a great success.

Sure enough, the Indian agent, who had ridden out with the escort and who was taking a great interest in the hunt, was first. He was closely followed by an Indian. The agent was riding a splendid gray horse and rode down all three of the bushes. He was good medicine. Understand—if the winner of the race should fail to knock down any or only one of the bushes he is considered bad medicine and the Indians will have little or no faith in him. So it is as necessary to ride down the bushes as it is to win the race.

By this time the women had the packs on and the procession started. I have often thought if I could only put this before the movie camera—as I saw it that day, stretched out on the plains for two or three miles—it would be great. But it would be a good job.

The third day, in the evening, we were signaled by the scouts that there was a large herd of buffalo near. They went into camp that night on a small stream called Hidden Wood Creek, about one hundred miles west of the Standing Rock Agency, off the reservation.

All was excitement and the camp was astir at daylight. The grinding of knives was going on at a terrific rate. The agent had brought five or six grindstones along. The knives could not have been ground before without interfering with the good medicine.

About 7 o'clock all was in readiness for the hunt. There were about 600 Indians mounted on their hunting ponies, stripped to the skin with nothing on but a breech cloth, belt and moccasins. Almost every Indian had a knife and most of them had guns. Some few had bows and arrows and spears. There was not a feather in sight on their heads. Their long hair was tightly braided and tied about the forehead with a buckskin string or a small beaded band of a bandanna handkerchief. As I saw these wild men seated on their ponies, eager and tense, I thought about the fact that these were the men that Custer met. Many of the men that were in the Custer fight six years before were in this hunt and what I saw was the same spirit and desire to kill that pervaded them on that day.

I have wondered if it would be possible for me to assemble a band of such Indians and get the spirit of the occasion before movie cameras. I know it cannot be done, as you cannot get the feeling there.

The Indians divided in two columns; one going to the right, and one to the left. They rode silently for about an hour, keeping in the draws and low places and out of sight. The buffalo were on a vast plain just to the west and the plain was covered for miles with them. They looked like a vast herd of black cattle. We estimated there were 40,000 of them.

The columns were about six miles apart when the Indians turned and rode into the buffalo. We were with the left wing. It was strung out for more than a mile when it turned and came upon the plain like well-trained cavalry. Not a word was spoken and not a shout was given until the guns began to crack. They rode down on them—silent, swift, terrible—and the slaughter was on.

I had killed buffalo and was watching the hunt as it continued through the day. The hunters were coming into camp until night. There was feasting and dancing. There had been enough buffalo meat brought in for the camp to feast. Two thousand buffalo had been slain and I stood and wondered at the amount of meat some of these Indians ate. I thought it would kill them, and some of them were sick the next day.

The next day was given over to the bringing in of the meat. Wagons, pack horses and travois by the hundreds were out. The women were all busy jerking the meat. No meat was wasted or spoiled. This was a hot day, about the middle of June. I never saw so much meat spread out on the ground, on bushes, on poles and on rawhide thongs that were stretched by the thousands of feet for the drying of this meat.

The women would take off the hide, which was not good for robes at this time, and then cut the meat into strips—the thickness of a good steak and a foot or more long. They had several big black kettles hung over a slow fire and this kettle was full of brine. I think the agent brought most of these things as he had a wagon almost fully loaded with salt. The women would take hold of one end of this meat and lower it into the brine and hold it there for a few seconds, then raise it out and lower it again and hold it about the same length of time. Then they would reverse it and dip the other end, after which they would hang it or lay it out to dry. The brine caused the pores of the meat to close up and the fly blows could not stick. But they still tried to keep the flies off as much as possible until the brine formed a slick, dry coat. There were patches of meat spread on the ground and the children were charged with the job of keeping the dogs from disturbing it. This meat on the ground had to be turned as soon as the top was coated.

The next day the hunt was again taken up and 1,500 buffalo were slain. McLaughlin, in his report of this hunt, says there were 5,000 buffalo killed but I do not agree with him. I think I am nearer right than he is. We stayed two or three days more and then lit out and in due time appeared at home.

How a Cheyenne Can Die

THERE IS AMONG THE Arapahos here a Cheyenne Indian named White Horse. His father was Two Moons, chief of the Northern Cheyennes and a leader in the Custer affair. His mother was an Arapaho woman named Sets in Front. White Horse spent his life with the Arapahos. He says he was born near Fort Fetterman on the North Platte River about 1875, which is about the time the Arapahos surrendered.[1] He went home to visit his father's people in 1890 and while there he was witness to a most strange and exciting incident. He related it to me as follows.

A white man had been killed by the Cheyenne Indians. He had been robbed and scalped and the authorities had asked the Indians to surrender up the murderer for trial by the white man's court. This incident happened near the Lame Deer Agency in Montana. The Indians, knowing who the men were, tried to settle the matter with the agent and the civil authorities. According to the Indian's idea of justice, compensation may be had by the payment of money. So they offered ponies, money and blankets to satisfy the claims of the white man. This was rejected, and more was offered.

Finally they were given to understand that Uncle Sam would not accept payment for the killing of another and the offenders

---

[1] Farlow refers here to the time when the Northern Arapahos agreed to settle on a reservation.

must be punished. They were told if the offenders were proven guilty they would probably be hanged. To this the Indians objected. They said they would never give up their young men to die in that way. They said it would choke the soul in the body and it could never go to the happy hunting grounds. They also said that the killing of a white man was justified at any time by the Indians as they would never kill enough white men to get even for all the Indians the white man had killed, or for the country the white men had taken from them.

Thus matters stood for a few days. Finally, troops were sent for and an ultimatum was sent to the Indians. When the Indians saw they must surrender their men to the white man or all be killed, they sent word the men would come in.

The names of the two Indians charged with the killing were Head Chief and Young Mule. They said they would show the white man how a Cheyenne could die.

The Indian agent's name was James A. Cooper and a company of soldiers had been sent to the agency to make the arrest. The two Indians sent word to the agent they would ride into the agency with their guns and weapons and would attack and kill anyone they found there. If the soldiers were there they would attack them. They set a day for this affair and all the country was notified of the event to be staged. All the Indians and whites for many miles around came to see the sight.

The Lame Deer Agency is located on a flat, surrounded by a low ridge. At the appointed time the two Indians appeared, mounted on their best horses, dressed and painted in all their finery. For the last two days they had been visiting and saying good-bye to their people. That morning they had been anointed by the medicine man of the tribe and prayers had been said for them. The night before there had been a solemn dance given for them.

The ridges surrounding the flat were covered with Indians and white men. The troops and Indian police were drawn up near the agency. When the two men saw the troops they put their horses at top speed and dashed straight for the soldiers, shooting and singing their death song. They rode at full speed in front of the troops and in the first volley from the troops one of them went down together with his horse. The other Indian rode on by, out of range. Then he turned and rode back. Again, the Indian was almost out of range when a shot brought him down. His horse was killed almost at the same time.

It was over and the Indian people came in and got the bodies. They buried them and there was much mourning for some time. The spot where these two Indians were killed is believed to be haunted and you cannot get an Indian to go there after dark.

※

White Horse came back to the Arapahos very much impressed by what he saw.

I have had White Horse out with me on several occasions and he is a very capable Indian. He played a leading part in the Metro-Goldwyn picture (starring Colonel Tim McCoy) called *War Paint* and did very well.

TRIP TO DENVER

I N JULY OF 1913 I took a band of thirty-five selected Arapaho Indians to Denver at the request of the Colorado Publicity League. The occasion was the annual conclave of the
Knights Templar and it was one of the grandest things I have
ever seen. There were reported to be 100,000 visitors in Denver
at that time and 20,000 plumed knights in parade.

They built a great amphitheater where the Civic Center now
stands. It had an area of about two acres and seated 25,000 people. They gave the Indians a camping ground just at the right of
the main entrance. It was seventy-five feet wide and 125 feet
deep and was surrounded with a six-foot-high wire fence. We
had eight tepees which we set up on the back end of our lot,
leaving a small open space in front.

After supper the first evening we built a fire. The committee that had engaged us also furnished us with some of those
little torpedoes to stick in the ground and light. They will
burn red for a long time and we had several sticking around.
When the darkness came on I had the Indians all stripped
down and painted up for a Wolf Dance. We put the dance on
around the fire. These Indians were gaudily painted, dancing
to the tom-tom and singing in the many-colored lights. This
made a weird scene and the people came crowding around trying to see us. They broke the fence down and closed in upon
us. We could scarcely move and we had to send for the police
to get us out of there.

There were 40,000 persons there and they were packed for two blocks. The police opened a trail and I told the Indians to follow me and we got away from the crowd. The police were unable to disperse the crowd until we were gone.

They fixed the fence the next day so that it would hold but we did not attempt to put on any more dances there.

While in camp we had three council talks with the committee that engaged us. J.M. Kirkendall was president and they would come to our camp. We would all go into our big medicine lodge for it was good medicine to transact business there. They told us the object and purpose of having us there. They said we were there as an advertisement for a great Indian show they proposed to put on next year. They proposed to have a representative number of Indians from every tribe in the United States assemble there in Denver next year and it would be called the Last Grand Council of the American Indians. They expected to have 1,500 Indians there and had already selected a beautiful campground at Inspiration Point. The Indians would be in camp for five or six months. In the forenoon they would have council meetings and the wisest Indians from all the tribes would talk. Many white men who were learned in the ways of the Indian would also talk. And, perhaps, the great white chief from Washington would condescend to address the Indians. We would learn much and find out how other Indians are living and would have laws passed for the betterment of the Indians. Then they would ask the Indians what they thought about it and some of them would make reply.

It looked alright but it was too big for the Indians and they did not understand it very well. But anything that gives an Indian a square meal and does not require too much exertion looks good to him. So they all agreed it was good.

All this was gone over again at the last meeting and some plans were talked of for the entertaining of the white people during the afternoons and evening. They were to put on their own games and sports and the white man was to be charged admission.

However, on account of the great war which was coming on then, the proposition was abandoned.

At this last meeting I noticed my old friend Goes-in-the-Lodge was a very earnest listener to all that had been said. He could not speak or understand a word of English and all our conversations were carried on through an interpreter. Goes-in-the-Lodge had sat beside me at all the council talks and had sometimes asked me in signs what was said. I asked him if he would get up and talk. After hesitating a moment he said "Yes, I will talk."

I said "Gentlemen, my old friend here, Chief Goes-in-the-Lodge, says he is willing to talk and I for one would be glad to hear him."

They agreed to this and I motioned to him to stand up and talk.

The old fellow arose, tall and straight. He was sixty-five years old. He looked around him for some time before he spoke. An Indian, when in earnest conversation, emphasizes the spoken word with sign language. Slowly raising his hands to the position of behind or after, Goes-in-the-Lodge said, "Too late, too late, white man's talk no good, too late."

Then, bringing his hands to the position of long time ago he said, "Long time ago, all this country belonged to the Arapahos and you may know this is true for they have their Arapahoe Street and Arapahoe Park and Arapahoe Boulevard—all because this was the former home of the Arapahos. They were happy people and their hearts sang each morning when they arose, for the country was rich. There was plenty of grass for their horses and for all the wild game to make them fat. There were lots of buffalo, elk, antelope, deer, fish and beaver in the streams—

everything to make the heart of an Indian glad. The white man came and that has been the death knell of the Indian.

"The day Columbus and his men landed we treated them kindly and asked them to go away. But they would not go away. They stayed, and more came. They killed our buffalo and burned the grass and cut down our trees and dug up the ground. Then we tried to fight them. No good. Too many white men. Too many guns. Indians kill one white man. White men kill a lot of Indians. They drove us out of this country and we went up north where it was cold and we had no home. The Shoshones would fight us there and the Crow Indians would fight us and the white man would fight us. The Sioux alone were our friends.

"For ten years we had no home and at last a lot of white soldiers and Shoshones came and surprised us and killed and wounded about half our number."[1]

After that, Goes-in-the-Lodge said, he held up his hands, put his thumb on a piece of paper, surrendered all his rights to home, country, liberty, and independence, and agreed to fight the white man no more.

"They put us on a little reservation," Goes-in-the-Lodge continued, "with our enemies, the Shoshones, where we did not want to go. And they told us to stay there and be good Indians and they would feed us. We did so and now they feed us no more. The buffalo are gone; the elk, the deer, the antelope, the fish and the beaver are all gone. The grass is poor and the Indian is poor. His heart is dead for he has nothing to live for."

Stretching himself to his full height, Goes-in-the-Lodge repeated: "Too late. White man's talk no good." And then he sat down.

---

[1] Goes-in-the-Lodge refers to the 1874 battle on Bates Creek, north of present-day Lost Cabin. See pps. 157-162 for details of that battle.

He told them much more of how the Indian had been driven back step-by-step by the white man and how they had hoped to hold this or that piece of ground where the grass was good and the buffalo were plentiful. But always they lost. He said "The white man comes into the Indian country and kills the Indian. The Indian never went into the white man's country and killed the white man."

He told them the truth as he had lived it. He was giving them history from the Indian's side as he had lived it.

⠶

While I am on this subject I will tell you how the Arapahos were driven out of Colorado. After General Connor's victory over the Shoshones at the Battle of Bear River in January of 1864 (for which he was promoted for slaughtering, starving and freezing most of the Shoshones under Sagwitch and Bear Hunter) Colonel John M. Chivington of Denver learned of the whereabouts of an Indian camp some hundred miles east. Securing a large body of soldiers and being well equipped, Chivington left Denver and marched to old Fort Lyons, about 65 miles east. There he recruited all the available troops. He had, in all, somewhat over 600 well-armed and well-mounted men and two mountain howitzers.

I am going to give you some of the Colonel's own report of this battle.

He says "On the morning of the 29th day of November, 1864 we surprised and immediately attacked a large village of Arapahos and Cheyenne Indians under Black Kettle and Left Hand. The Indians, although surprised, hastily formed in line of battle and stubbornly resisted." Mark these words: *stubbornly resisted.*

Chivington continues: "They were driven down the creek a distance of five miles when all resistance was abandoned and they fled precipitately. The pursuit was continued until night.

We secured about 500 horses, ponies and mules and after securing a large amount of Indian trophies of Indian life and warfare, their village was destroyed."

He says, "About 600 Indians lay dead on the field."

His next statement is, "It is perhaps unnecessary for me to state that we took no prisoners." Read between the lines. This report is on file in the war department. What did they do with the babes, the old, the sick, the crippled and wounded?

He says, "There were about 900 Indians in the camp." And in this he is very close to the right number.

"About 600 lay dead and we took no prisoners." No Indians ever lived that did not run away.

He says, "The next day the pursuit was again taken up." What was he pursuing? Women and children. There was not an able bodied man who escaped, as they fought the advancing soldiers, trying to save their loved ones and shouting for them to run for the horses. All the men and many others were slain.

Chivington's pen fails to tell what he found in the pursuit. The route of flight taken by these poor, frightened, cold and frozen women was dotted every mile by the body of some unfortunate one who could go no farther. Those who could go no farther were left behind. They were as a flock of chickens with a hawk after them. They fled, each for themselves, and could care for or help no one.

Chivington says, "Our casualties were eight men killed." And yet he tried to dignify it by calling it a battle.

He says, "After having marched 100 miles through two feet of snow and my men and stock being exhausted, we returned to Fort Lyons."

※

Let me tell you what the Indians say of this engagement. It was told to me by Goes-in-the-Lodge, Plenty Bear, and Black

Coal—all Arapahos. Two of them were in the fight and Black Coal was in the camp of Little Raven when the fugitives arrived. He says that less than 200 of the Arapahos reached Little Raven's camp alive out of the 900 who were in the camp on Sand Creek when it was attacked that winter day.

Goes-in-the-Lodge said the troops surprised them at the time and place mentioned, but did not attack them. He said the soldiers told them to surrender. All the soldiers were lined up and had two big guns pointed at them[the Indians]. He said the Indians were very much afraid. Goes-in-the-Lodge was then fourteen years old and he has a very clear recollection of events at that time. He said the Indians were told to bring their guns and lay them at the feet of the two men who stood out in front on their horses, one of them holding a flag. The Indians did so. Most of their guns had been brought in when the shooting started. Goes-in-the-Lodge does not know how the shooting started but thinks that some of the young warriors refused to bring their guns in and perhaps shot a soldier. He said he heard some of the young men say they would never give up to the white man.

Anyway, all at once, all the soldiers began shooting and advancing on the village. Goes-in-the-Lodge's father shouted to him to get his mother and run for the horses. The men all grabbed whatever weapons they had left and tried to stop the soldiers, but they could not. Goes-in-the-Lodge got his mother on a pony and he also got on one and they fled as fast as they could. Many of the women and children were on foot. The snow was about six inches deep and they all traveled—everyone for himself. Many of them could not go any further and were left behind.

They traveled that night and the next day and night. They came to a patch of brush and there were a lot of frozen rosebuds on the bushes. The Indians were very hungry and they ate the buds and small twigs. They also killed an old horse that was about played out and got some fires going. Some of them lay down by the fires and fell asleep. It was very still and cold and they could hear things a long way off.

Goes-in-the-Lodge thinks it was about 9 o'clock when they heard the sound that brings joy to the heart of every patriotic American and is to me the sweetest sound on earth—the sound of a bugle far away in the still of the night. So the Indians fled into the darkness and did not stop again until they reached the camp of Little Raven, forty miles away. There was one young woman with a baby who was so weary she could not rise up and they left her sitting by the fire. Goes-in-the-Lodge thought the soldiers must have gotten her as they never saw her again.

Now to compare the two stories. Colonel Chivington says he immediately attacked them and that there was two feet of snow. The Indian says Chivington had gotten most of their arms before he attacked them, and there was six inches of snow. As to the reasonableness of the two statements: if there had been two feet of snow there would not have been an Indian who escaped for they could not have walked. And some of them carried babies forty miles. It is also reasonable to suppose that the Indians could have killed only eight soldiers with such weapons as they still had in their possession—spears, bows and arrows. It is not unreasonable to suppose they would have killed more soldiers if they were fully armed and were attacked in the open such as in the Custer engagement.

The report of the battle and the conflicting reports brought in by those engaged in the affair created quite a furor in the press reports and the newspapers at that time. An official investigation was demanded and held by the second session of the 38th

Congress to see if it was honorable warfare such as the government was supposed to wage on the Indians, or a horrible massacre as many thought. The affair was white-washed and no report ever brought in. Colonel Chivington received no credit for the Battle of Sand Creek, as it is called.

THE ARAPAHOS COME TO
THE RESERVATION

THIS WAS THE LAST OF the Arapahos in Colorado and most of the survivors of this battle went south with the Southern Arapahos, as they are now called. But a few of them joined the Northern Arapahos under Black Coal, Sharp Nose, Friday and Water Man. These Indians were again hit by General Connor's command on his Powder River campaign. Colonel Coutant says in his history of Wyoming that General Connor had an army of about 400 well-equipped men. On July 20, 1865 he left Fort Laramie and joined his command. The general rendezvous was to be on the Rosebud. He issued strict orders for his commanders to keep scouting parties on their front and on their right and left flanks. One paragraph in these orders attracted great attention in the east. It read, "You will not receive overtures of peace or submission from any Indians, but will attack and kill all male Indians over twelve years of age."

Looking at the orders issued to the armies in the field in pursuit of the Indians you can arrive at but one conclusion: [they called for] the annihilation of the American Indian.

The entire regular army, or at least most of it, was afield in pursuit of the Indian. General Sheridan was in command in the field on the frontier and summed up his opinion in these words: "There are no good Indians but dead Indians."[1]

---

[1] General Phil Sheridan vigorously denied ever having said words such as this, but few historians have taken his protestations seriously. Those historians

General Sherman was at the head of the army of the plains and said, "The Indian must be suppressed by merciless and vindictive warfare."

With this condition facing the red man is it any wonder he retaliated with all the fiendishness and cunning in his power?

Again I quote you from Coutant about the Powder River campaign of General Connor. He says, "On August 29th, 1865 as they were marching up Tongue River, they discovered a large Indian village about noon, just in the act of leaving camp. Some of them had already started and many of them had not yet taken their tepees down. They were Arapahos under Black Bear and Old David." Without going into details of the battle he reports 63 warriors were slain, about 1,100 ponies were captured and a large amount of their stores and village was destroyed. He says, "Several of our men were wounded, three or four afterwards died of their wounds."

After this these Arapahos were in exile with no place to call their home for ten years. They roamed from the South Pass on the Sweetwater down to the Platte, and on the head of the No Wood and tributaries of the Big Horn River. They were with the Sioux much of the time, who were their friends.

※

About the 25th of June, 1874 there was a raid made on the ponies of the Shoshone Indians on their reservation. The raiding parties came to within three miles of Fort Washakie. There was a dance going on among the Indians at that time above the post

---

have disagreed however as to when he said it. Most convincing is the story told by Captain Charles Nordstrom. Nordstrom claimed that Sheridan was approached by a Comanche Indian at Fort Cobb in 1869. The Indian struck his chest repeatedly and declared, "Me, Toch-a-way; me good Injun." Nordstrom said Sheridan gave a quizzical smile and answered, "The only good Indians I ever saw were dead."

and the ponies were not missed until evening. The raid was reported to the commanding officer Captain Bates, who took the matter up on behalf of the peaceful but very indignant Shoshones. He said he would help them recover their ponies and also punish the invaders.[2]

With 165 armed Shoshones under Chief Washakie and his own command, Bates took up the trail of the raiders on the third day and followed it for about 100 miles. They discovered the camp of some Indians who had evidently watched their backtrail for several days but, thinking they were not pursued, were not on guard at this time. So the surprise was complete.

Early on the morning of July 4 the combined forces of Chief Washakie and Captain Bates attacked the Indian village—Arapahos under Black Coal and Sharp Nose, successors to Black Bear and Old David who had since died. The battle lasted for about four hours and the Indians retreated into red rocks that stood near their village and refused to be dislodged for some time. Finally they all fled, leaving the white soldiers and Shoshones in possession of the village where they camped for the night. Three soldiers were killed along with three or four Shoshones.[3]

The Arapahos, numbering about 700, were badly whipped and nearly half of their number were either killed or wounded.[4]

---

[2] Captain Alfred Elliott Bates wasn't as anxious to seek a confrontation as Farlow suggests. The feisty little Phil Sheridan, then a lieutenant general, happened to be at Camp Brown when these events unfolded and it was he who ordered the pursuit of the Indians. Camp Brown's post surgeon, Thomas Maghee, wrote in his journal that Sheridan "is a small, heavy-set man with a little gray in his hair and a good deal of whiskey in his stomach."

[3] Two soldiers died in the battle. Three soldiers and one officer were wounded. Two Shoshone Indians fighting the the Army troops also died.

[4] There is some disagreement about the number of Arapahos in the village when it was attacked by Captain Bates' force. Farlow's estimate of 700

It is reported there was a large party of their best men out on a buffalo hunt at that time of this battle and if they had been in camp the fight would have been different.[5]

This battle is known as the Battle of Bates Creek. The stream was named after the battle. It is a tributary of the No Wood, which is a tributary of the Big Horn and is located about one hundred miles east of Lander.

A very peculiar circumstance happened at this battle. When the attack began, a warrior by the name of Red Turtle grabbed his gun and ran out. He called to his wife to get the children and run for the rocks. The mother, taking the youngest (a boy of three years) in her arms, told the older boy (about seven years old) to hold on to her dress. With her arms full she ran out of the lodge. When they were outside young Red Turtle saw the soldiers coming and shooting. He let go of his mother's dress and stood watching the fight. He later told me he stood there until the soldiers were very close. All at once he got scared and, looking for his mother and not seeing her, he dove into the brush. The stream was heavily lined with a thick growth of willows. He crawled in as far as he could and was well concealed.

Arapahos is on the very high end. Most reports say there were 112 lodges in the camp which would suggest that there may have been 400-600 Indians. One source placed the number of lodges as low as 11 or 12.

The most reliable count of Arapahos killed comes from tribal elders who were interviewed about the battle some 60 years later. They named seventeen men, women and children who died in the battle. Military reports claimed twenty to twenty-five killed.

[5] At the No Wood River ranch headquarters of the Noble & Bragg Sheep Company, the log cook shack was one decorated by a skull which had been found on the site of the Bates Battle. The skull had a bullet hole in it and it was tacked above a pair of crossed beef bones. A sign below it read, "Meals—thirty-five cents."

He lay there all day until night. He said he could hear the white men and Shoshones talking but he kept very still.

After darkness he crawled out. He said he passed very close to the soldiers but lay very close to the ground and crawled very slowly until he was out of sight in the darkness. He went back of the rocks where he knew his people had gone. Not finding them there, he took up the trail. In order to find which way they had gone he felt for the pony tracks and in this manner he followed until daylight when he could see he was on the right trail. All day long he followed. He said he went to sleep twice but would wake up and waddle on. All he had to eat the second day was a nest of young birds which he ate raw. He later told me how the blood ran out of the corners of his mouth.

The evening of the second day, just at sundown, the Indians saw Red Turtle trudging along in the distance and came to him. He was all in. The Indians had fled for a distance of about 35 miles. Finding they were not pursued, they had stopped to care for their wounded and bury their dead. Little Red Turtle had followed and is alive and well today. He often tells me of this battle and if that is not the instinct of the wild, then I don't know.

This is the battle Goes-in-the-Lodge had reference to in his talk to the white men at Denver.

Little Shield told me that after the battle they sent word to the commanding officer at the fort on the Shell River (meaning the Platte). He meant either Fort Fetterman or Fort Robinson. They asked the officer if there was any place on earth the Arapahos could go that the white man would not surprise them and kill their women and children. This was the third time they had been so slaughtered; first on Sand Creek by Colonel Chivington's men, next on Powder River by Connor's men, and last by Captain Bates and the Shoshones.

They surrendered and were placed on the Shoshone Indian Reservation in 1878.

I was there when the Arapahos were coming in and it was hard for the Shoshones to keep from fighting them. Had it not been for the great Chief Washakie and his complete control over them, they would have driven the Arapahos off the reservation in a short time. They have never been friends and are not friends today, which is just fifty years since the Arapahos came here.[6]

The Arapahos camped down on the Platte and around Fort Robinson for a few years after they surrendered and signed the peace treaty. In fact, Little Shield and his following did not move in on this reservation until 1882.

There is not a single case of intermarriage between the two tribes and they still speak disparagingly of each other. The Shoshones hold the Arapahos in contempt and call them beggars and say they have no home—only what the Shoshones

---

[6] After the battle on Bates Creek the Northern Arapahos struggled for survival. They successfully resisted government efforts to place them on the Sioux reservation because they feared they would lose their identity. And they also resisted efforts to place them in Indian Territory (now Oklahoma) with the Southern Arapaho because Sharp Nose feared sickness and disease in the warmer climate. They sought their own reservation north of the Platte River and, preferably, along the Tongue River near present-day Sheridan, Wyoming. Arapaho warriors enlisted as scouts for the military in order to gain influence with the whites. While serving with General George Crook's forces, these Arapahos found themselves working together with Crook's Shoshone scouts. And it was this contact that brought about enough of a peace that the Arapahos could eventually be placed on the Shoshone Reservation.

In the fall of 1877, an Arapaho delegation went to Washington and received assurances they would be placed on the Shoshone Reservation. They spent that winter on the Sweetwater River in the vicinity of Independence Rock and began moving onto the reservation in the spring of 1878.

have given them. The Arapahos cannot help themselves as they have no other place to go.[7]

❈

The placing of the Arapaho Indians on the Shoshone Reservation is one of the many strange doings of the Interior Department. The two tribes were hereditary enemies and the Shoshones helped Captain Bates whip the Arapahos into submission. The Shoshones did not want them. The Arapahos did not want to go there. It has been an unpleasant situation for fifty years and still it exists. But it is too late for any change now.

Washakie often spoke to me about the Arapahos and wondered when the government was going to take them away. When I asked him if he did not consent to having them on the reservations he said, "Yes, only they said it was only for a short time and until they could get another reservation for them."

I have read the treaty between the Shoshones and the United States and after describing the boundaries of the reservation its says "All the land laying within the above described boundaries is hereby set aside for the exclusive use and benefit of the Shoshone Indians and such other Indians as the government may from time to time desire to place thereon, with the full and free consent of the Shoshones."[8] I asked Washakie about this and he said that he did not understand all of the writings of the

---

[7] More than fifty years after Farlow wrote this manuscript the tribes remain socially and culturally distinct. In 1968, there were only 63 enrolled Arapahos who were married to Shoshones.

[8] Actually, the treaty says the land is "set apart for the absolute and undisturbed use and occupation of the Shoshone Indians...and for such other friendly tribes or individual Indians as from time to time they may be willing, with the consent of the United States, to admit among them."

white man but he remembered something of this. But he thought it meant a stray family of Indians, not a tribe. No, never a tribe, and particularly not a tribe that was their foe, as he put it, a tribe that he could not shake hands with. And this would be a natural interpretation.

When the Arapahos continued to stay on the reservation and all the Indians of the two tribes drew their rations and annuities at the Shoshone Agency, there were near riots two or three times. The Arapahos were openly abused and insulted by some of the younger Shoshones. So a sub-agency was established 32 miles down the Little Wind River where the Arapahos were to receive their supplies. This arrangement was much better. This place was called the Arapaho Sub-Agency.[9] Eventually, the Arapahos had their own boss farmer and carpenter and blacksmith, the same as the Shoshones.

When an allotting agent was sent in here to allot lands in severalty to all the Indians, Washakie openly remonstrated. But no attention was paid to it and the Arapahos were allotted lands the same as the Shoshones. They participated in all the benefits of the reservation equally with the Shoshones and have continued to do so. These benefits include the monies received from the sale of hides and for leasing and oil royalties.

I was telling U.S. Senator Kendrick of this condition and told him the Shoshones should at least be paid for that portion of the reservation that had been taken away from them and given to the Arapahos. He replied that it was one of the plainest claims of the Indians that had been brought before the Committee on Indian Affairs since he had been in Congress. He

<hr>

[9] This is the place which is known today simply as Arapahoe.

introduced a bill in Congress to bring this matter before the Court of Claims and now the bill has become a law. There is no doubt but what the Shoshones will soon be paid for this land.[10]

---

[10] Omaha attorney George Tunison worked with the Shoshone Indians for many years to bring about an equitable settlement for the government's placement of the the Arapahos on the Shoshone Reservation. In 1927 the U.S. Congress cleared the way for the Shoshones to file a court claim. And finally, in 1937, the Shoshones won their suit and a judgement of almost $4.5 million from the U.S. government. In return, the Arapahos became equal partners with the Shoshones and the name of the reservation was changed to the Wind River Indian Reservation.

1904 TREATY WITH THE SHOSHONES AND ARAPAHOS

THIS RECALLS TO MY mind the making of a treaty with these Indians in 1904.

James McLaughlin, U.S. Indian Inspector, and two or three other gentlemen were sent in here to make a treaty for a part of this reservation as the Indians had indicated they would sell a part of it to the white man. I had met McLaughlin before and was pretty well acquainted with him. He made the remark at that time that he was opposed to these bread and beef treaties, as he called them. However, the government proceeded to have double rations issued to the Indians and they were given plenty of beef and coffee so that for two weeks they would have plenty to eat. All they would have to do was to eat, drink and be merry.

While the negotiations were going on, the entire personnel of both tribes were camped around the agency and the young folks had a good time.

The proceedings went on very slowly. The first day or so was spent in getting the boundaries of the land they proposed to sell laid out. Many very solemn speeches were made by the leading Indians who wished to impress upon the rest of the tribe the tremendous importance of the transaction. They cautioned that the Indians should not be hasty and should give the matter very grave study before acting.

After two days of counciling, the boundaries were definitely fixed and the price was the next thing. Jim Atkins (a white man married to a half-breed Shoshone) and myself were listening in on the proceedings.

After two more days of feasting and talking, the committee representing the United States offered the Indians $400,000 in cash for the land—about a million acres. The gentlemen making the offer went to great lengths to try to show the Indians how much money this was.

An Indian's idea of money is gauged by the silver dollar. The government representatives told them how many squaws it would take to carry this money on their backs, allowing each squaw thirty pounds; and how many ponies it would take to carry it, allowing each pony one hundred pounds. The amount was too big for the Indians to comprehend. It looked to them as if they would have about all the money they would ever want. So the matter was settled for them to begin to sign the next morning.

In the morning, Atkins and myself were in the little room back of the store that the committee members were using for their office. There were also three or four Arapahos in there at the time with James McLaughlin. Lone Bear, chief of the Arapahos, asked me what I thought of the treaty and I told him that I had nothing to say.

McLaughlin saw the gesture of the chief and guessed its meaning as the question had been asked and answered in the sign language. And McLaughlin could talk signs.

I consider that James McLaughlin, at the time of his death, knew more of the plains Indians than any other man that ever lived. He and I have often talked of the Indian situation. I remember one of his visits to this reservation when he was telling me of some change they were going to make. I jokingly remarked that the government is reducing the Indian to civilization. He replied, "I believe you are more than half right."

McLaughlin, getting the question asked me by Lone Bear, spoke up and said, "Mr. Farlow, I have seen these Indians ask you a couple of times what you thought of the treaty. They seem to have great faith in your judgement and you have refused to answer. I myself would like to hear your opinion."

I replied, "Well, Mr. McLaughlin, since you have asked me for my opinion I feel free to give it. I have refrained from expressing myself for I might have changed the opinion of some of the Indians and this is my opinion. The government sends its shrewdest and ablest and most experienced diplomats out here to treat with these Indians. They are clearly outclassed in that respect. You have been trying to show these Indians how much money $400,000 is and it is beyond them and they think it is enough. I will say this. You are offering these Indians this money for an empire. If this body of land belonged to a party of white men you could not buy it for four million dollars."

I turned and walked out.

The Indians were not asked to sign this treaty and immediately a new treaty was drafted and offered to them the next day. It was signed and it is the present treaty.

To show what McLaughlin thought of the land, the treaty signed did not buy the land from the Indians. Instead, the government acted as agent for the land and it took on an entirely different value. Instead of twenty cents an acre, the price they were originally going to pay the Indians, they offered this land for sale to the white man in tracts of 160 acres at $1.50 an acre. That price was valid for the first three years and then was reduced to $1.25 an acre for the next two years. Then the balance of the land was offered for sale at a minimum of $1.00 an acre.

The Indians have received more than $400,000 from this land already and have only disposed about one-fourth of it. The rest is now leased to the stockmen of this vicinity for grazing purposes and the Indians receive rent of about $40,000 a year, or about eight percent on $500,000.

Soon after the treaty was concluded I met McLaughlin in Lander and he thanked me for making the talk I did. He said it made him realize in an instant that they had driven too sharp a bargain with the Indians. He said my reference to the white man brought the idea to him of selling it to the white man and not to the government.

McLaughlin is one of the grandest men I ever met and was a great friend of the Indians.

FIRST WILD WEST SHOW

I T WAS ABOUT THE year of 1894 that we held the first wild
west show in Wyoming that I have any knowledge of. This
was in Lander and it was my first experience in using the
Indians as showmen. I had quite a lot of trouble convincing
them they were not to hurt anyone in the sham battles with the
whites. Many of them wanted to shoot the whites with blunt
arrows which would be very painful. I was afraid some of the
cowboys would retaliate with a sixgun, as there was not a very
friendly feeling between the two at that time.

At this celebration we put on the first relay race I can
remember. We used five horses each and ran each horse a mile.
And after each horse had run a mile he rested while the other
four made their run. Then each horse ran another mile as it was
a 10 mile race. It took a mighty good horse to run a mile and
then repeat after resting about ten minutes. There were three
strings of horses in this race.

We had such a good time at this celebration that we concluded to make it an annual affair and in 1908 we had one of the best
celebrations ever. At that time Charles Erwin [Irwin] of Cheyenne
was just breaking into the game and he came up to our show with
a carload of running and bucking horses. Famous among them
was Old Steamboat, then in his prime. At this show we put on
relay races, stake races, hat races, wild horse races, and mess wagon races. One event in particular that has never been done very
successfully since then was the burning of a man at the stake.

During a lull in the track events there appeared an old trapper at the far side of the arena—a circular half-mile track—riding slowly. He had a couple of coyote hides tied on his saddle. As this was the 4th of July he was wearing just a shirt and overalls with an old bandanna handkerchief around his neck and a slouch hat. He had long unkempt hair. Soon there appeared in the distance a band of Indians and they took after him. Whipping his horse to full speed he came in front of the grandstand which was well filled with an enthusiastic audience. All the people within a hundred miles around used to come to see these shows.

The Indians were close upon the trapper when he suddenly veered to one side and made for his cabin which was standing in the middle of the arena. He barely got inside as the Indians closed in on him. His guns began to bark through the portholes of his cabin and Indians began to fall. Soon the ground was strewn with dead Indians, all killed with blank cartridges. The Indians then fell back and laid low while one of their number crawled up behind a bunch of brush that was near the cabin and, throwing a lighted torch on the cabin, succeeded in setting it afire. The cabin and the grass and trash around it had been saturated with coal oil so when the torch fell on the roof the fire started. The trapper stayed in as long as he could stand it and then ran out right into the arms of the waiting Indians who captured him. Then they decided to burn him at a stake which had already been set about one hundred yards from the cabin.

The prisoner was dragged to the stake and securely bound—or so it appeared. He was facing the audience and held the ends of the ropes in his hands. The Indians—seventy-five Arapaho warriors in all the glory of war paint and feathers— were a fine sight in themselves. After tying their prisoner they brought out the tom-tom and began beating it. They fell back about twenty feet from the prisoner and began a war dance.

This continued for about two minutes and it gave the audience a view of a real war dance. The Indians would dance up to the prisoner and threaten him with their tomahawks and knives and then dance around wildly.

The prisoner was writhing and tugging at his bonds and at last he got loose and started to run. Then he tripped and fell right into a pile of brush and straw that had been gathered for the purpose of burning the prisoner. By a prearranged plan with the Indians, when the trapper fell he unbuttoned the top button of his overalls and shirt collar. Two Indians grabbed the bottom of his overalls and pulled them off and another Indian stripped off his shirt. Still another Indian smeared his face with paint and he himself grabbed a war bonnet that was concealed in the straw all this time. The Indians were gathered around him so closely that the audience did not see what was going on and in the brief time of ten seconds the change was made.

Under this pile of brush and straw was a dummy made and dressed exactly like the trapper. So finally the trapper stood as a full-fledged Indian and brought the bogus trapper to his feet. Three or four other Indians roughly dragged the dummy back to the post while the Indians were wildly yelling and dancing. As soon as the prisoner was brought to the stake and before he was fairly tied the Indians had the brush and straw piled high around him. Screeching and yelling and waving their tomahawks they lit the fire in three or four places and in an instant the trapper was enveloped in flames.

When I saw the excited condition of the Indians I at once gave the signal for the cowboys and soldiers to charge. They were waiting and the plan was for them to charge, disperse the Indians and rescue the prisoner. That at least was the audience's perception of the act. When I gave the signal for the rescue party, I pretended to believe the Indians had gone wild and were really taking the life of the trapper. I frantically yelled for the boys, "For God's sake, hurry." The Indians, when they saw the soldiers and cowboys coming, sprang for their horses and rode away just as the shooting and shouting rescue party arrived.

In the excitement of the battle the trapper was burned up. The brush and straw and clothing had all been piled at the foot of the stake and nothing remained but the burning body of the trapper. No one knew what became of him and there were screams and cries from the grandstand. Many women went into hysterics. It almost broke up the show.

If they had watched closely they would have seen two Indians riding away on one horse. Stub Farlow was the trapper and rode out of the fight behind Chief White Horse.[1]

This show lasted for three days and when it was over Charley Erwin remarked, "I have learned how to put on a wild west show."

He returned to Cheyenne and the next year he was at the head of affairs at Cheyenne. They put on the best show they had ever had and called it "Frontier Days." They got the name we had been using for several years copyrighted. Cheyenne has continued to put on a great show and today has one of the best wild west shows in the world.[2]

❦

Among the Arapahos is a white man called Whiteman. When I first met him in 1880 he was about twelve years old. I met him and two Arapahos riding bareback. When I met them and saw he was as fair as I was I spoke to him and said, "Hello,

---

[1] Stub Farlow was Albert Farlow, one of E.J. Farlow's two sons.

[2] Cheyenne's event was being called Frontier Days since before the turn of the century. And there is no evidence that Lander's event ever was called Frontier Days. Farlow's claim that Lander originated the name appears to be unfounded.

On the Farlow Ranch E.J. Farlow is shown at center dehorning cattle with the help of his sons Jule (left) and Stub. (Photo courtesy of Pioneer Museum, Lander.)

boy. What are you doing here?" He just looked at me and I soon found out he could not speak a word of English. But he could converse freely in Arapaho.

I got well acquainted with him after this and have known him ever since. He married an Arapaho squaw and still lives as an Indian.[3]

He was captured when he was a baby and was raised by old Sun Road and finally married one of his girls. I have had him out with me on several occasions and he is a good show Indian and can sing and dance as well as any Indian in the tribe.

---

[3] Sharp Nose described Charlie Whiteman as one-third Ute, one-third Arapaho, and one-third white. He was born to white parents but was captured by Ute Indians during an attack on a wagon train in the 1860s. Later he was captured from the Utes by the Arapahos. Tim McCoy said Whiteman could speak some English but was more comfortable speaking Arapaho. He was accepted as a full-fledged member of the tribe and served as a member of the Arapaho business council from 1935 to 1938 and from 1943 to 1944.

GOES-IN-THE-LODGE

I WANT TO TELL YOU something of my old friend Goes-in-the-Lodge. This is a strange name and means nothing but a joke to most people. But let me tell you how he got this name.

In a battle on Powder River in 1866 the Arapahos attacked a Crow camp that had invaded their hunting grounds. In the night Nock-a-Cha, as he was then called, went into one of the lodges of the Crows and killed two men. You may know it takes a little nerve to go stooping into the lodge of an enemy and get him, and so the name.

There is a pretty legend connected with Goes-in-the-Lodge as to how he got his wife. As it was told to me, the Arapahos were camped on the North Platte (they called it Shell River) in 1872 and there was a beautiful Indian maiden in the village. Many of the young men were sparking her. One fine morning in June there were three or four of the young warriors laughing and talking with her on the edge of the village when a small band of buffalo came down to the river to drink. They were no more than a half-mile away. In the bunch was a magnificent bull. It could be seen quite plainly and was distinguished by its immense size as compared with the rest of the band.

The girl laughingly said, "The man that can slay that buffalo with a knife and without a horse, I will marry."

The young men shouted and laughed at such a good joke, all but Goes-in-the-Lodge. He was silent for a moment and after gazing intently at the buffalo for a short time he started for his

*One of E.J. Farlow's closest friends among the Arapahos was Goes-in-the-Lodge.
This is Goes-in-the-Lodge's identity card for his participation in movie prologues
in London.* (Photo courtesy of St. Michael's Mission.)

tepee. He soon emerged from it stripped of everything but his
breech cloth and moccasins, and a belt with his knife in it.

He started after the buffalo which had left the river and were
slowly going out on the plains. When they saw the Indian, they
galloped off. Nock-a-Cha followed and hour after hour he pursued them until they began to tire. The weaker ones began to
drop out until he was following the big bull alone. The bull
would turn and make a rush at Goes-in-the-Lodge who would
evade him. After a few of these charges, Goes-in-the-Lodge
watched for his chance and, springing on the buffalo, he grasped
a firm hold in his shaggy hair with his left hand while he drew his
knife with his right hand and stabbed the immense brute repeatedly in the heart and lungs. The bleeding buffalo soon staggered
and fell. Goes-in-the-Lodge cut out his tongue as a trophy.

There was a large number of Indians who had gotten on their horses and followed to see the finish of the chase. They skinned the buffalo and Goes-in-the-Lodge had the hide in his tepee for many years. He got the girl and she is living yet and they are proud of each other and are a fine old couple.

I always take Goes-in-the-Lodge with me on any and all of my trips as he is faithful and honest.[1] He is always willing to help with anything we have to do. But he smiles with the other Indians when the director of a motion picture tries to tell them how they should do something he knows nothing about.

---

[1] Farlow refers here to his numerous trips with Indians from the Wind River Reservation to appear in movies and in live prologues to movie presentations. Details of these trips appear in later chapters.

FREIGHT AGENT

B EFORE THE RAILROAD built into Lander the nearest railroad point was Rawlins on the Union Pacific, 135 miles away. In 1887 the Chicago & Northwestern Railway built to Casper and we began trailing stock there. Casper was 150 miles from Lander but there was a better trail for stock.

Then, in about 1895, they began hauling freight from Casper. In the days before the railroad all the goods and supplies for the merchants, saloons, ranchers, stockmen, the military post and the Indian agency were hauled in here by horses, mule and ox teams. Wool and some crops were hauled out the same way. This gave work for about fifty men and about 500 head of stock. The freighting was done mostly in the summer as winter weather sometimes closed the roads for long periods of time.

My brother Zeke drove and owned a good sixteen-horse team. Many of the men drove this size team with four wagons loaded with 16,000–20,000 pounds of freight.

In the summer of 1896 the freighters of the valley organized the Freighter's Union and tried to do business in a business way. But they could not seem to get together and were continually trying to cut each other out of a load. In 1903 they had their annual meeting in Lander and twenty-eight of the best teamsters were present. They asked me to the meeting and asked me if I would be their agent. After some talk I consented. I told them that I would run the business end of it and they were to do the hauling. There would be only one head, and that was me.

Unless they would all agree to haul and obey me in every way, I would not start. They all agreed.

I at once got busy and saw all the merchants, saloon men, wool growers, the men at the fort and agency. I told them I would do their hauling when they wanted it done and they all agreed.

We fixed a schedule of prices for through freight and local. The price was $1.25 per hundred pounds for through freight from either Rawlins or Casper to Lander, and fifteen cents more to the post or agency. The price was one cent per hundred pounds for all other hauls over fifty miles. Under this distance it was one and a half cents a hundred.

I had fifty freighters enrolled under me. They hitched up 500 head of stock and loaded about half million pounds at one time. We handled six million pounds of freight during the year of 1903. Three and a half million pounds of this was wool and it was hauled an average of over 100 miles.

At that time Casper got the most of the wool. Casper was the largest receiving point for wool from the range in the world that year, receiving over ten million pounds. These freighters were the finest body of men it has ever been my good fortune to work with and there was no confusion. They went where I sent them for a load without a murmur. I worked with them only one year as my own business demanded my attention. When the railroad built into Lander in 1906 all this hauling was stopped. The teams scattered, looking for new fields.

WOLF ROUNDUP

I N AUGUST OF 1917 the wolves and coyotes were very bad in Fremont County and did great damage to the flocks and herds of the stockmen. At a meeting of a number of stockmen it was decided to have a wolf roundup and I was selected as president. The handling and management was largely turned over to me.

I took an inventory of the population and the material for the roundup and found that by enlisting the services of the Indians, cowboys, ranchers, sheep men, herders, camp movers and the young folks of the towns of Lander, Riverton and Shoshoni, I could rally a force of about 600 riders. So we drew a line around a piece of badlands lying east of Lander and south of Riverton and Shoshoni. It was about thirty miles across and was infested with coyotes, wolves, badgers, rattlesnakes, horned toads, deer, elk, antelope and thousands of wild horses and cattle. We were organized in eight companies of about seventy-five riders each. Many of the riders were girls and it was to be the greatest holiday of the year.

The companies moved out to their positions on the line the day before the roundup. In the morning they were to divide and go to the right and left until they reached the end of the line of the next company. In that way the bad lands were surrounded. By 7 o'clock the next morning the circle was about eighty miles in circumference. There were about eight riders to the mile at the start. They were to start for the center at exactly 7 o'clock

The Farlow Wolf Roundup produced no wolves but it was a monumental event that required much planning and some investment. This certificate shows that E.J. Farlow received twenty-two shares of stock although it is not apparent if he purchased the shares or received them as payment for his efforts in the planning of the event. (Photo courtesy of Pioneer Museum, Lander.)

and would gradually come closer together as they came to the center, driving everything before them. They were to advance on a walk and would reach the center about noon, having about fifteen miles to ride. This would be great fun for the young folks.

They had a very good time but they bunched up too much and lost quite a lot of stuff. We found out that you could not drive the antelope. There were hundreds of them inside the circle and they would drive for two or three miles and then break through the line and go back to their range. Some of them passed through the line when the riders were not more than twenty feet apart and the boys could almost touch some of them.

When the riders all arrived at the center we had a large corral to drive this stuff into and this is what we had: one elk, twelve antelope, 100 coyotes and bobcats, one bear, about 500 head of cattle and 2,000 head of horses. We had a movie camera there and got some very good pictures and had them finished up.[1] Mr. Delfelder[2] gave them to a film company of Sheridan, Wyoming by the name of the Northwestern Film Company. Their secretary was a Mr. J.E. Maple but we have never heard of him or the films since.

We had all the automobiles for a hundred miles around in the badlands that day. It was hot and dry and most of the riders camped at the corral that night.

The roundup was not an entire success but we learned a lot about driving wild animals. The boys and Indians killed a large number of coyotes on the drive and all told we got rid of quite a lot of them. There were at that time about three million sheep in Wyoming and it was estimated that the coyotes were killing about two percent of these annually. So you see it is quite a loss and does no one any good.

The biological survey is doing good work now in this state in the destruction of these pests and the price of furs is an incentive for trappers to try to get them. A good coyote hide is worth $15–$20 and three or four hides a month is good wages.

They called this roundup "Farlow's Wolf Roundup." The Indians got a great kick out of it and would have liked to have it last a week as they were just getting started good in one day. It was against the law to kill antelope but they got a number of them that got hurt in the drive and they had to kill them.

---

[1] Actually, there was a movie production company in attendance at the wolf roundup. But the results seem to have been disappointing. Some time later an effort was made to stage action that could be combined with footage of the actual event. But still the results were less than satisfactory.

[2] J.A. Delfelder was one of the major sheep men in the Wind River country at this time. Much of the area covered in the Wolf Roundup was his range.

TRIP TO CASPER

I N 1914 I TOOK seventy-five Indians and about twenty-five cowboys and cowgirls to Casper and helped them put on a very good three-day celebration. An incident occurred here that frightened the Indians.

The committee had engaged an aeroplane to come there to give exhibition flights and it was the first aeroplane the Indians had ever seen. It landed in the arena. When it took off it had to run straight for our mess tent, which was a 24'x40' eight-foot wall tent. It was new and strong and well staked down with half-inch guy ropes. The cook was working in the tent when he heard the roar of the flying machine and he stepped outside to see what was happening just in time to avoid being hit. The machine could not rise and was about two feet from the ground when it hit the tent. It was luck for the aviator for just beyond the tent was an eight-foot iron fence and a solid wall. The tent stopped the force of the machine. The plane was badly damaged.

They had the plane in the same starting position the next day and started the engine. My Indians like to broke their necks getting out of its direction, and they pronounced it no good.

In 1916 I took twenty-five selected Indians to Fort Collins to help them with the celebration there. For many years before and after this I had Indians in force at Lander, Riverton and Rawlins and assisted them in some of their own celebrations at home.

THE COVERED WAGON

I T WAS IN THE middle of September in 1922 that I received a call on the phone from the Noble Hotel at Lander. I was home and preparing for bed when I answered the phone. It was Colonel Tim McCoy calling and I went to the hotel.

He said, "Dad, I have the biggest Indian proposition I know of and I want you to help me. They want five hundred Indians to make the movie *The Covered Wagon*[1] and we have been turned down by the agent at Fort Hall in Idaho. You can handle this if anyone can."

This flattered me very much.

I told him the Indians were working on the roads and on a ditch. And, as many of them had crops that were not in yet, I thought about one hundred was all we could get here. However I knew Agent Donner at Fort Hall and called him up in the morning to see if he would not help us.

I told Agent Donner who I was and he remembered me so I told him what it was that we wanted and asked him if he could

---

[1] Based on an Emerson Hough novel about the Oregon Trail, the movie *The Covered Wagon* began with a production budget of $100,000. But soon that budget jumped to $500,000, an almost unheard of amount for the time. Eventually the total cost ballooned to near one million dollars. The end result was a colossal (for the time) ten-reel movie. It grossed more than $3.5 million and that made it one of the top five grossing films for at least ten years after it was made.

spare us some Indians. He said, "Sure I can, but the man they sent here could not get any. He did not know I was agent here."

I told him that Colonel McCoy was by my side and he would come there as fast as he could and help get them. I would gather what Shoshones and Arapahos I could get and meet Colonel McCoy in Salt Lake.

This we did and we were taken to Milford on the Salt Lake line. From there we were hauled in trucks across the desert for sixty miles to the filming location, which was not far from Ely, Nevada, just over the line in Utah. Here we worked until the nineteenth of November in the making of that great picture.

Some amusing things occurred during the making of this picture. I first met Ernest Torrence here and his actions and work in the picture reminded me so much of Jim Baker who I was well acquainted with and I called him Jim Baker in my mind. Here I learned that the director and assistant director do not need any advice from anyone. One night they were putting on a night scene in which the emigrants were having a dance and they had the big lights on the scene. Vernon Keys was directing it. They were to dance the Virginny Reel. He got them all up before the camera but they did not know how to dance this Virginny Reel and they milled there for some time. Finally the Colonel came back to where I was and asked me if I knew how to put it on and I said, "Yes, to the queen's taste." He went up to Keys and told him and I saw Keys cast a glance at me and continue. So I went to my tent which was nearby and retired. Some time later I heard old Bill Jackson calling the dance but he did not know how to call it.

A few days later the order went out for all the emigrants to hitch up and get ready to corral their wagons for the great Indian fight. They had 225 wagons, the finest wagon train I ever saw. Under the direction of James Cruze and two assistant directors they pulled down on the flat in a big circle and stopped. Cruze

One of the first major films to feature Indians from the Wind River Reservation was the epic The Covered Wagon made in 1923. Here, part of the cast of that movie poses with Wind River Reservation Indians on location near Milford, Utah. E.J. Farlow is seen seated at left. Colonel Tim McCoy, who worked closely with E.J. Farlow in coordinating movie appearances by the Indians and who later became a movie star in his own right, is seen seated at right. (Photo courtesy of Pioneer Museum, Lander.)

and the camera were on the hill with a splendid view. Cruze said, "Now all you drivers, when I fire this shot, turn your teams and drive straight to the center of the circle." The drivers did as told and they had the worst mix-up you ever saw and had to unhitch some of the teams to get out. It took them until noon to get straightened out.

"That ain't right," said Cruze. "Be back at 1:30 and we'll try it again." At noon the Colonel came to me and asked me if I knew how to corral wagons.

I told him I did but said "You keep still and let them go, they don't need anyone to tell them."

He would not keep still and told Keys. After dinner, when all was ready on the hill, the Colonel and Keys rode up to me. Keys very politely asked me if I knew anything about parking wagons. I told him "no" and I noticed his lip drop. The Colonel seemed disappointed.

Keys said that they were having some trouble getting the wagons in position for the big fight.

I asked, "You mean corralling wagons?"

He brightened up and said, "Yes, you might call it that."

"How do you want them corralled? In stockade formation or battle formation?" I asked.

"Battle formation, if it can be done," he replied.

"It can be done easy enough, but I am not running the wagon train. Mr. Fouch is running it and I would not think of telling him what to do. I did not ask him to tell my Indians what to do," I said.

About that time Jim Cruze and Jim Fouch came up and Cruze said, "Dad, can you help us out in this matter?"

I told him I would and asked him how many wagons he had. He told me 175 as they had dropped off fifty. I told him to bring them on.

I corralled them in battle formation, banked solid, wheel-to-wheel to resist an attack and we did it the first time. We had only three wagons left over which were drawn inside as this is the way to dispose of any extra wagons.

James Cruze seemed to appreciate what he got and thanked me. I felt all swelled up.

Trip to London

WHEN *The Covered Wagon* was finished I took the Indians home.

The picture looked so good to the producers that they decided to open it in the Grauman Egyptian Theatre in Hollywood with an Indian prologue. I selected all of the Indians for the prologue but unfortunately could not leave home at that time. The prologue was a great success but the Indians got tired and quit after only about three months. Colonel Tim McCoy called my son Jule and he brought the Indians back to Lander.

The prologue went over so big in Hollywood that the Famous Players Lasky Company decided to open the picture in London with the same prologue. I was in Yellowstone National Park at the time and I received a telegram from Hollywood asking me if I thought it possible to take the Indians across the big water and I answered that I thought it could be done. They wired me back as to the price for the Indians and my services.

In the meantime I had been figuring the cost of sending a man to London and return and it looked to me to be a financial impossibility. So I thought I would kill the project. I wired back that it would cost five dollars a day for each Indian and $200 a week for myself and all expenses.

The next morning there was a telegram under my door telling me to go at once and secure the Indians. All arrangements for our transportation would be made.

I took the next coach for Lander and reached the agency about five o'clock the next day. I asked the driver of the bus to pull over to the agent's office as I wanted to see him just a minute.

Paul Haas was a very good agent and a mighty nice man. He said "We have been expecting you, but I can tell you the Indians will not go. The Paramount people wired me and I have had it up in council with both tribes and they decided it was too dangerous. The Famous Players Lasky Corporation has also wired the agent at Fort Hall in Idaho to see if the Bannock Indians would go and after two days of counciling they decided not to go."

This is what met me on the start. Jimmie Moore, the post trader and a man who had spent his life here, said, "I will bet you the best hat in the store they don't go."

I told the agent I was sorry they had covered the ground without consulting me but said, "With your permission I will call the Arapahos together and see what can be done."

He replied to go ahead and that I had all the authority over those Indians that the Commissioner of Indian Affairs could give me. He wished me luck.

I got on the bus and came on to Lander and sent word down to Arapahoe, which is a little station on the Chicago & Northwestern Railway, fifteen miles northeast of Lander. It is the heart of the Arapaho settlement on the reservation. I told them I would be down in the morning to talk to them. They were always glad to talk when they thought they were going to get to go someplace with me.

So in the morning my wife drove me down and when I arrived there quite a number of Indians had gathered around. But the occasion was not so much to see me as it was on account

E.J. Farlow had to do considerable work to convince Wind River Reservation Indians to cross the Atlantic for movie prologue appearances in London and Paris. And when the trip was about to begin, a large contingent gathered at the depot in Arapahoe to say goodbye. Here Left Hand (center) and an unidentified Indian pose before they board the train. (Photo courtesy of St. Michael's Mission.)

of a sick Indian—Old Painted Bear—who was dying of old age. They had him in a tepee and painted for death. They were beating the tom-tom and chanting the death song to keep the evil spirits away and were just waiting for his spirit to take flight.

When I spoke to any of them of the trip they said they did not want to talk and that they had settled it in council.

I realized that I could do nothing there. The train was coming along at this time going east and I boarded it and went to Casper. They were having a rodeo there and 125 Arapahos had driven down from the reservation, taking their villages and ponies. The Casper committee had told them they would pay them wages equal to the railroad fare. I got there on the last day of the rodeo just as it was finished. When the Indians saw me they gathered around me and shook hands with many "hows." They were very glad to see me.

One woman, Mrs. White Plume, came to me crying and said her husband had died. They had him in a house downtown and wanted $125 for embalming him and putting him in a coffin to send home. The Indians had no money and she was on her knees to me with her arms clasped around my knees, telling me what a good man I was and what a great friend of the Indians I had always been. I helped her up and told her to be ready to go on the next train. I would pay the bill and have her husband on the train and would also wire them to meet the train at Lander. She blessed me and thanked me with "Na Ho, Na Ho" (meaning "Thank you, thank you").

I told the Indians what I had come for and they said that had been settled. But I told them I was coming out to their camp in the morning to talk to them and that it was not settled with me.

So in the morning I went to their camp and they all met me. Yellow Calf, their leader and a very good talker, got up.

Talking with a word of English now and then but using the sign language to emphasize his statements, he said that his boy had gone to school to read of that country in the book. He told them it was the same as an island, with water all around it and that big boats were many days going there—maybe eight, maybe twelve days. Long time no see land and maybe no see stars and come night and all see is water. Maybe cloudy and no see sun and maybe that big boat miss island and go on and never come back. He said he had heard white man say that big boats go out and never come back. Long time ago, a white man, long hair, long mustache and whiskers (meaning Buffalo Bill) took a lot of Sioux Indians across the big water and in coming back one Sioux died and they threw him in the big water. He wound up his talk by saying that no Arapaho would ever be thrown in the big water if he could help it.

He sat down and that was what I had to go against.

I got up and began, using the sign language, some Arapaho and some English. I told them that old Yellow Calf was the same as an old woman. He was afraid, same as a little baby. I roasted Yellow Calf until he got mad and the rest of them were laughing. I reminded them of all that I had done for them in so many ways, in sickness and in death.

They assented to all this with loud grunts and hows.

Then I told them they would go with me on the railroad and it was more dangerous than the water. I told them they had much better boats now and this story of getting sick on the water was just told to frighten children, that men did not take it seriously. Finally, I said I was going across the big water and was going to leave my wife and family home; that I was not going into any danger; that I was going to take some Indians with me—maybe Sioux, maybe Shoshones, maybe Arapahos—but I had come to the Arapahos first as they were my best friends and I had known them the longest. I told them I knew they were not all afraid and that there were some brave men among them. At that I saw some of them begin to straighten up.

I continued in this line for a short time and then old Goes-in-the-Lodge got up. He said that all I had told was true and that I had been their good friend. He said that he and I were the same as brothers. We had worked together branding cattle and horses and we had rode the range together, had ate and drank and slept together. Holding up one finger he made the sign that he would go. Then, holding up two fingers, he made the sign that his wife, too, would go with me across the big water.

Then Black Weasel got up and said he would go and his wife would go.

The ice was broken and I took them across the big water.

When I had them all ready to take the train I went down to Arapahoe. Old Painted Bear was dead and they had the death smoke coming out of the tepee. I was not at all sure they would go. I got there nearly an hour ahead of the train and we had a private baggage car for our tepees and baggage and this they loaded very reluctantly. After I had gone to see the bereaved family I gave Big Head, who was sort of a public announcer, five dollars to get out there and tell the rest of them that some of them were going away and to wish them well and so on. He made a very good talk and all was ready. But the train had not yet whistled. So I gave Black Horse ten dollars and told him to take it out to Big Head who was just about to quit talking. I told him it was for the family of Painted Bear from me. That gave him something more to say.

Then the train pulled in and I began to hustle them on board. A big, fine looking Indian named Buffalo Fat put his foot on the step to get in the car but then stepped back and said he was not ready to die yet and refused to go. Then Mrs. Black Weasel hesitated. I told her to get on and don't be a baby. I was surely glad when the train pulled out. This was on the 12th day of August, 1923.

When we arrived in Chicago we had a 5-hour layover and I took them to Lincoln Park. The things that interested them the most were the elephants and the monkeys as they had never seen either of them. The elephants they called a big hog with a tail on both ends. One of them kept looking around and asked me if it had eyes.

Yellow Horse came to me as we were leaving the park and said in the sign language that he had seen five little animals that were half white and half dog. I did not know what he meant. I asked him again and he said the same thing. Black Horse (who could talk good English) came up just then and I asked him what Yellow Horse meant. He told me it was the monkeys. That is what they called them: half white man and half dog.

When we arrived in New York we camped in Central Park. The crowds came around us and annoyed us very much. We had police to guard the camp but they were not able to keep the crowds back. When we were not there they would pull up the back of the tepees and some things of the Indians were stolen.

We stayed in New York a week and appeared on the stage at the Criterion Theatre, Colonel McCoy taking the stage and presenting the Indians.

The day before we sailed they gave us a day off and I paid the Indians $1,000 in wages. They all wanted to go shopping. They had told me at the theatre the night before that Macy's big store had about everything and it would be as good as any. So the next morning I called up the Macy Company store and asked for the manager. I told him that I had twenty-six Indians who had $1,000 and they wanted to go shopping, but only six of them could talk English. I asked him if it would annoy him if I brought them to his store. He said, "No, bring them down by all means."

We were camped at 82nd Street in Central Park and when I told him where we were camped he said, "Take the elevated and get off at 32nd and Broadway and I will meet you there myself."

This he did and we went into the store and divided the Indians in groups of five or six and put an interpreter and a salesgirl with each bunch. But it was soon necessary to put a policeman with each bunch as the crowds gathered around them so they could not move.

The manager and I were following a group, watching them. He was about as much interested as anyone. We came to one of these elevators or traveling stairways and were just ready to go above. But we were waiting for a couple of Indians who were looking at an article nearby. Old Red Turtle and his wife were standing very near this stairway and did not see it. One of these busy New Yorkers came pushing through to the stairway and Red Turtle, in stepping aside to let him through, stepped on the stairway. He started heavenward. His good wife began to gaze at him and he at her. I was standing ten feet from the stairway and soon his gaze raised enough to see me. I never saw such a scared look on an Indian's face.

I was watching him from the start and knew he was scared and had my hand extended, closed, in the sign to stand still. The sign is made by lowering the hand slightly. He understood. Then I extended the two first fingers and turned them to the right and left, which meant to look around. He looked at the man beside him and then the other way and back to me. I raised the fingers up for him to look up. By this time his head was level with the upper floor and he saw them getting off. He began to crouch and get ready. When he was up he made a big jump and got away from the elevator. Then he straightened up with a great sigh of relief and looked down at us. I told him to stay there for we were coming up. But his wife had discovered the elevator and would not get on. I had to take a firm hold of her arms and push her on.

We shopped until noon when the manager asked us to have lunch with them. Of course we accepted and we were the guests of the store and had an elegant lunch. After lunch we went on top of the building and there were photographers and reporters there. The Indians and the manager were photographed together in many pictures.

It was three o'clock when I asked them if they were all through buying. Some of them said no, they had not spent all their money. So six of them went shopping in charge of two girls. I kept the rest on the sixth floor in the corner.

In an hour the rest came back—all but two who had got lost. The girls said they went away while they were looking at some beads. I went with one of the girls and soon I saw a big crowd. Above the crowd I could see the feathers of a war bonnet. I had found my Indians. They were Yellow Horse and Left Hand. Neither of them could speak a word of English. I pushed through the crowd and got near them without being seen. Yellow Horse was at the silk counter and was holding up and admiring a gorgeously flowered pair of $26 silk pajamas. They would have been immense in a wolf dance.

I backed away and told the girl to bring the two Indians when they were through. I returned to the rest of the Indians. Soon the girl came with them and it was now 5 o'clock. The manager told me that the front entrance and Broadway were terribly congested and if we took the freight elevator it would put us out on an alley just across the street from a subway entrance.

When we stepped out of the elevator on the street I told them, "Now you have been in automobiles, on the surface here and you have been on the railroad up in the air (meaning the elevated). Now we are going down in the ground and will get on a railroad there and ride to our camp."

Old Goes-in-the-Lodge looked at me and then stepped out in the street and stamped his foot heavily on the ground as if to test it. He shook his head and said I was talking crooked. In other words, he did not believe me.

I said "Come on."

The store had sent a boy to guide us and he led us across the street. We went down the stairs and our train was just pulling in.

We scarcely stopped. We went very fast and their only concern was that the train might come to the end of this hole too sudden and not be able to stop. Soon the conductor said, "Your station, sir."

We got out and came up a couple of flights of stairs and there, not more than a block away, we could see the tops of our tepees.

Old Goes-in-the-Lodge looked around and exclaimed, "Waugh, all the same prairie dog, go down in one hole and go a long way and come up out of another." They were ready to believe anything then and one of them asked me if there was a road under the big water to London.

Our boat—the Baltic—sailed at noon on August 18th. The company had put all our baggage on board except the hand baggage. I had got each Indian a good grip and had his name put on it in big black letters. So after an early dinner we were hauled down to the pier and then marched along the wharf to our boat. As we were walking along I could hear them talking in their own language and looking at the tug boats that were moving in the harbor and wondering which of them they were going on. One saw a very large and fine boat and exclaimed that he hoped that was the one we were going on. They did not see this great boat at the pier.

About this time the camera men who were always shooting us motioned to the Indians. They had their cameras on the boat and just at the end of the gang plank. I told the Indians to look up, we were going to be shot. They knew what I meant and braced up. We walked up the plank which, at that time was nearly level, and past the cameras.

The camera men, shouldering their cameras, said "Bring them off again as we want to get them going on." I had them follow me and we went back on the wharf and again marched past the cameras. One camera man told me to take them below as he wanted them going down and out of sight.

During the London trip, E.J. Farlow was photographed in a park with a group of Indian women and children who made the trip to participate in movie prologues. The women are left to right Alberta Sitting Eagle, Judith Bell, a woman identified only as Bill Shakespeare's mother, Lambro, unknown, and Mrs. Red Pipe. The children are unidentified. (Photo courtesy of St. Michael's Mission.)

This we did and then we were right among our rooms. One of the cabin boys, seeing Red Fox with his grip in his hand, said "Mr. Red Fox, let me take your grip, this is your room right here."

Red Fox could not speak English very well and said, "No, we are going on boat."

The boy said, "You are on the boat now."

At this the Indians began to jabber in Arapaho and we went on deck and they looked around. To the right for a hundred yards was all boat and to the left the same. They began to wonder how it could move.

By this time the people were coming aboard pretty fast and the great Majestic steamed out past us with flags waving and bands playing. Its thousands of passengers were waving hands and handkerchiefs. I told the Indians we were going to run that boat a race across the big water and that interested them. But we never saw the Majestic again as it was a much faster boat than ours.

That afternoon and night and the next day the trip was much as I had told them it would be—nice and smooth. But the second morning our ship was rolling.

The cabin boy said to me, "If you will just lay still and keep your eyes closed, you will not be so sick as the sight of the rolling boat tends to make one sick."

I did as he told me but each roll of the boat made me heave a little more and soon my supper and everything else was up.

I came on deck about nine o'clock and there in their corner were my Indians. Some of them were sick but they could plainly see that I was sick too and it did them a lot of good to see that the Big Chief was sick.

We had been told that we would be across in six days. But when the six days passed and we did not see land, and when the seventh day was well along and we still had not seen land, the Indians began to be very uneasy and asked me questions.

One of the questions was, "How can they tell where we are, as we have not seen a star or the sun for two days?"

I replied, "By the compass."

"How does the compass know?"

When the boy told them they would be in sight of the Irish coast in the morning, every Indian was up before daylight and out on the deck and waiting to see land. And they were happy again.

We landed at South Hampton and were taken by train to London where we camped in the Crystal Palace Grounds. It was a great park with several buildings in it.

A man had a little show going on and it was called "The Far East." It had a fortune teller, a spider woman and a few other tricks. There was a big sign which said "White Buffalo, an American Indian." My Indians were very curious to see him. I asked the attendant there who he was and he said, "I don't think he is an Indian." I told my men I would take them all to this show sometime and they could see him.

We were making two appearances a day at the London Pavilion Theatre at Piccadilly Circus and they had a great electric sign up there that said "The Centre of the World." I guess that was right.

Three days after we arrived I took them to see "The Far East." The manager had told me to bring them up at any time and walk right in. It would not cost us a cent as the crowd would follow us in. He would announce his attractions until he got a few inside and then put on his show as he had no regular time for it. The Indians marched in and sat down well in front on a long bench. They had, in fact, the front seats. The show began and the fortune teller told some wonderful things and the magician made things appear and disappear until my Indians had their eyes bugged out a foot. Then came White Buffalo with his war bonnet on. He was a little yellow Negro with a chicken feather war bonnet. When he stepped out on the stage and looked down on my warriors sitting there like statues, his eyes rolled and he stammered and could hardly do his stuff. He was looking at some real Indians and I guess he realized what a poor excuse he was. After a few days he quit his job because my Indians ridiculed him so.

When we arrived at the theatre, the manager, Louis Nethersole, a younger brother of the once internationally famous actress and singer, threw up his hands when he saw the financial size of this prologue. It consisted of twenty-seven Indians including children, Colonel McCoy and myself. He said the picture would never carry it. He had never had but two pictures run two weeks in London. One was the *Birth of a Nation* and in seven weeks it fell flat. The other was *Robin Hood* and in six weeks it fell as there were not seventy-five paid admissions.

When we left Lander we had a ten week contract to appear on the stage at London and the company had the option of extending that time to six months.

We started in playing to crowded houses. In fact, the seats were sold for two weeks ahead. We appeared on the stage for ten weeks and then signed for ten weeks more. Then we signed for five weeks more. We were twenty-five weeks on the stage at Piccadilly Circus.

At the end of three months the picture was released in Paris and they wanted an Indian prologue. So we split the Indians and I took four of the men and three women and the children to Paris and opened the picture in St. Madeline's Theatre.

I could not take the stage as I could not talk French and so all I had to do was to wrangle drunk Indians and keep them sober enough to appear on the stage when wanted. We had a man to introduce them—a Canadian Frenchman who called himself White Elk. He looked as if he might have a little Indian blood in him. He had been employed by the management to take charge of the Indians and appear on the stage. He met us at the landing as we got off the boat from crossing the channel and rode with us to Paris.

He was broke and touched me for ten shilling as soon as he met us. He was a good mixer and a big failure as a man but he had been playing the cabarets there and going big in his turkey feather war bonnet. An Indian notices a bonnet as quickly as a woman and anything but eagle feathers in a bonnet is as calico to silk in a dress. You will see the look of disgust and contempt on their faces when they see these cheap imitations.

I was expected to get these Indians located and trained sufficiently and acquainted with White Elk so I could return to London after three days and could attend to my duties there. But on the third night, after the show, White Elk took two of the Indians to a night club and all were drunk the next day. I had a time to get them sober enough for the two o'clock performance. White Elk was the worst one of the three and was not going to appear at all but I finally got them on in some sort of costume.

I wrote to London that day that instead of getting a man to care for the Indians I had got another Indian on my hands. So I stayed there three weeks.

I was just going to get a good trip over the battle fields of the world war when I got a wire from London to come at once— Indians on warpath. I got a train and caught a boat and arrived in London about seven P.M. and went directly to the Indians. We had them at that time in a small hotel at Russell Square as the rainy season had set in and the tepees were wet. Some of the Indians had got colds and they were afraid of the flu.

When I arrived there I found the Indians all there and sober, but not dressed for the stage. I asked them what was the matter

A caption which read "Paris sees a new brand of American tourists: Indians from the Plains" appeared with this clipping from a Paris newspaper. The photograph was taken as E.J. Farlow and a group of Wind River Indians arrived in Paris to present movie prologues. Farlow is shown in a dark overcoat at left center. (Photo courtesy of St. Michael's Mission.)

but I could not get a word out of them. They said only that they had quit.

I asked this and that one but they would not talk. At last I said, "Someone is in the wrong here, either you or the company. If you go home I am going home with you. We all go together. But you must give me time to find out what is wrong. I always do what is right with both Indians and white men. Dress up and go with me to the theatre tonight and I will find out what is wrong."

After some talk they went with me and appeared on the stage as usual. This was a Saturday night and we had no appearance on Sunday so I paid them their wages.

On Sunday I took them out to Hyde Park and they watched the nobility ride. The titled ones were pointed out to us and the Indians greatly enjoyed seeing the Englishmen ride bobtailed horses in their English saddles.

They came home in great good humor and we went on the stage that night. I told them I had not seen the boss yet. They kept on and after a few days I got to talking with Lodge, White Bear and Black Horse and about all I could get out of them was that McCoy did not know how to handle Indians.

When we were in Paris I took the Indians to many places of interest—Cathedral of Notre Dame, Cathedral of Sacred Heart, Arc D'Triumph, Tomb of Napoleon, Eiffel Tower and others. But they were not interested in these. We went up in the Eiffel Tower 750 feet and stopped and some of them complained of being cold and some of being sick and one was afraid. They all wanted to go down and they were very glad when we were on the ground. One of them said he did not see why any man would want to build a building like that as it might fall over and kill somebody.

In London I took them to the London Museum, the zoo, Tower of London and many other historic places. But it was too big for them and they didn't know anything of the history of the country. The things that would interest them were a monkey on a string or some trivial thing they had never seen before.

Red Turtle was deaf as a post and someone told him he could get an ear trumpet and that would make him hear. So he bought a very good one. I think he paid four pounds for it and he hung it around his neck. He would put one end in his ear and they would speak in the other end and he could hear very well.

Red Turtle's wife was as deaf as he was so, taking it to their tepee, he told her to hold it to her ear. She did and he began to talk to her and she heard so well that it frightened her. She would not try it again. He told me the next day that she took it and put it in a box they had and locked it. She said she was afraid it would be talking in the night. Red Turtle was always getting into trouble. He is the little Red Turtle who survived the Bates Creek Battle of 1874.

I took them to Madame Tessaud's Wax Works in London, one of the greatest places I have ever seen. The wax figures were so perfect you could easily mistake them for the living person. The Indians were very much awed by them and called them ghosts. We got along pretty well until we came to the Sleeping Beauty. She was a beautiful girl lying on a couch, slightly draped and sleeping. Her bosom was rising and falling as if gently breathing and it was perfect. The Indians looked at her intently for a moment and Red Turtle touched her hand. It was wax— cold and clammy—and he turned and left. The rest of the Indians followed him and that was the end of the wax works. I could not get them in there again.

I was greatly interested in the Old London Tower. I stood by the block where Mary, Queen of Scots was beheaded, saw where her head had fallen on the ground and where her life blood ran.

I stood in the room where the two little princes were slain, saw the crown jewels and many other historic things.

In my contact with the Indians I have had several close calls and my wife says, "They will kill you yet." But I think my good medicine is still good. I was never more afraid than one night in London. You may not know it but when an Indian gets whiskey he gets crazy and wants to kill. There are many instances of this and they often kill their best friend. Henry Read, my best Shoshone friend, got drunk and killed his wife and himself. Several others have done the same. There is now in the courts at Lander two cases of first degree murder charged against Indians for killings while drunk. Ambrose Old Man killed his friend Dominick Crook while drunk.

I have gone among them when they are drunk and they have said, "You are our good friend. We like you, but you are white and the white man is no good down in his heart." They hate the white men and when they are drunk it comes out.

One night in London, about midnight, the janitor of the hotel came to my room which was about a block away and said, "The Indians are on the war path."

He wanted me to call the police but I had told him if there was any trouble to call me. I dressed and went over and they were still in their stage clothes of paint and feathers and tomahawks and spears. And they were drunk. They had been quarreling among themselves.

When I opened the door and looked in on the bunch of half-drunk Indians they were quiet and eyed me like a snake. The authorities took my gun away from me when I landed in London as no one carried any weapon there. But at that time I wished for my old gun. They respect a good gun when they know a man can handle it. But I dared not hesitate. Yellow Horse was standing in the center of the room and had a big bottle of whiskey that only a few drinks had been taken out of. I stepped up to him and grabbed him by the shoulder with one hand and the bottle with the other. I said "Come with me."

I started up the stairs with him as his room was the second floor above. I called to Goes-in-the-Lodge to follow me which he did. I was sure I could depend upon him. I so surprised Yellow Horse that he came right along for the first flight of stairs and then he began to hang back, but not bad. I got him to his room and, pushing him down on the bed, told him to stay there. I told Goes-in-the-Lodge to keep him there and I would attend to the rest.

I came down the stairs and they were all standing there watching my every move. I think they thought I had a gun under my coat and I said, "Now you fellows go to bed, I am surprised at you acting like this and getting that old man drunk."

I acted as if I thought they were all sober. "Now boys, get to bed and get some sleep for I have a big treat for you in the morning." I often had treats for them as we were continually invited out to a dinner. We could get a great feast and the Indians enjoyed these very much.

We left London for home on March 1st, 1924 on the Cedric. We stopped a week in New York and then came home. This is the longest time I have ever had Indians away from home. In the last twenty years I have had Indians off the reservation twenty-seven times. There were never less than eight Indians and sometimes as many as 150. I have had them to Denver twice, in Fort Collins, in Casper, in Rawlins, Salt Lake, San Francisco, Los Angeles, Cheyenne, Hollywood, Omaha, Chicago, New York, Boston, Philadelphia, London and Paris. And I have never lost an Indian or had one seriously sick.

The instance in Casper when White Plume died and I was not there was to my credit, for they not only lost White Plume but were never paid a cent for their trip and they are sure if I had been there they would have been paid and White Plume would not have died. They would have been paid alright if I had been there because the first thing I look out for is the pay and I don't go until that has been cinched.

The government is very careful of the Indian now that it has him whipped and on little reservations. It is difficult to get Indians off the reservation and an ordinary person asking for Indians will be promptly turned down. It is against the policy of the Interior Department as they claim it interferes with the civilizing of the Indian and keeps alive the old songs, dances and traditions. Will Hays is a pretty big man in the movie world and, when any of the big companies want Indians, Will Hays can step in and smoke a cigar with the Indian Commissioner and get almost any Indians they want.

For my part, I claim it is the greatest education for the Indians. They learn more on one of these trips than they would in a lifetime on the reservation.

The government has set a form of permit for taking Indians and it reads like this. Addressed to some Indian Agent or Superintendent, it says you may permit the Famous Players Lasky Company (or any other company that is asking for Indians) to take such Indians as you can spare without interfering with their agricultural or domestic pursuits, for such a time and such a purpose as is asked for. Said Indians are to be accompanied by some person that is trustworthy and reliable, acquainted with the needs and wants of the Indians, and entirely satisfactory to the Indians themselves.

This is where I come in as they always ask for me to accompany them. They came very near not going to Hollywood for the prologue of *The Covered Wagon* without me. Goes-in-the-Lodge insisted that I go.

They are to be properly fed and cared for and properly transported. Medical attention, if necessary, is to be provided. They shall be kept away from all evil influences and intoxicating liquor and finally returned in good order and condition and paid so much wages. A bond is then given for double the amount of the probable cost of the trip and you can go.

I find this bond is a good thing for it protects me as well as the Indian. If we should get stranded anywhere I would immediately notify the commissioner that the Indians they permitted so and so to take were neglected and abandoned by them. Then the government would proceed at once under the bond to return them to the reservation.

TRIP TO YELLOWSTONE

IN OCTOBER OF 1924 I was called upon to take a band of twenty Indians to Yellowstone National Park for Indian and buffalo scenes in the movie *The Thundering Herd*, a Famous Players-Lasky production. But I was unable to go on account of having a very sick mother at my home. So I sent my son Jule with them.

After getting them all together at Arapahoe, I talked to them and told them to go with him and do good work and obey him. I said I would hear a good report or a bad report and any Indian that did not do well or made any trouble could not go with me again. Jule took them and they had a splendid trip.

Among them were Goes-in-the-Lodge, Medicine Bird, Night Hawk, Painted Wolf, War Chief, Round Chief, Night Horse, Tepee Chief, Bad Teeth, Rising Buffalo, Old Eagle, Lone Bear, Bear Eagle, Big Ribs, Black Wolf, White Bear, Two Strikes, Tallow and Nea Ah Thaw (called White Man). They were all fine Arapaho warriors.

They took the Burlington train at Shoshoni and went to Gardiner, Montana at the north end of the park. From there they were hauled by truck to the Buffalo Ranch on the Lamar River. This was paradise for the Indians. Never in their wildest dreams had they pictured such a scene. There, on the open hills and scattered along the river in the grassy bottoms and lying by the riverside, were buffalo by the hundreds, elk by the hundreds, deer and antelope by the hundreds, and coyote and a few black and grizzly bears—a hunter's paradise and an Indian's heaven. They were to hunt and kill those buffalo for the movies and never had they had such a treat. They could taste again the buffalo meat. They were given horses by the company and for two weeks they were used in the scenes depicting the hunting and chasing of the buffalo. You can see them and the buffalo in that great picture of Lasky's, *The Thundering Herd*.

Goes-in-the-Lodge told me it was the best trip he had ever had and said he did not want to leave those buffalo. It made him wild again and he wanted to go off in the hills and camp again where he could see nothing but the mountains and the sky and the wild game and live over again the life he was born to. When the old man finished speaking he sighed and turned away as the recollections of the wild, free life of the Indian came back to him.

In January of 1925 I was called upon again to send the Indians to California to finish this picture and for some other work. But again I could not go as my dear old mother lay paralyzed in my home and it was a pleasure and a privilege for me to do all in my power for her in her last days.

We can never repay that dear mother for all she had done for us. She died in June in her 91st year. Although I was a gray-bearded old man of 64 years, I was her boy just the same.

Jule went again with the Indians and they were in California for a month. They were sent home then and called again in April for a prologue for *The Iron Horse*, a Fox production that opened in the Grauman Egyptian Theater. Colonel McCoy took the stage with them.

E.J. Farlow is shown at center with his wife Lizzie (second from left). Also shown are E.J. Farlow's son Jule (third from right) and his wife Rosalie and three of their four children. Family members are uncertain of the identifications of the three children. (Photo courtesy of Pioneer Museum, Lander.)

THE THREE BAD MEN AND
A TRIP TO PHILADELPHIA

IN THE EARLY PART OF September in 1925 I was at the Jackson Lake Lodge when my son Jule drove up in a car. He was working for the Fox Corporation at the time and said they were camped about fifteen miles from there on Snake River. They wanted me to go with him to the camp. There were quite a lot of boys there that I knew and they were glad to see me. I had a pleasant evening.

The next day they were going to Jenny Lake, a distance of about five miles, to shoot *The Three Bad Men*. I went along to see them work.

The three bad men came riding out of the brush and dashed into Jenny Lake Creek which was about 150 feet of swimming water. They sat erect on their horses and had them loaded down with guns. They had a big heavy saddle slickers and coats tied on the horses and the riders were big men. I knew what was going to happen when they hit swimming water but it is a high crime to say a word when a director is putting on a scene.

They were too heavy for the horses and when they hit swimming water the horses began to feel for bottom. One man grew faint-hearted and turned back before he hit swimming water. All the time the Canadian Mounted Police were pouring a hail of lead (blanks) at them. One splendid horse of Jack Moore's tried to swim but was going deeper with Ed Jones.

I yelled, "Ed, get off or you will drown your horse."

This he did and his horse came across.

The other man pulled his horse over on himself and almost drowned both himself and horse. But they both got out.

After warming themselves by a good fire for a few minutes and a good shot of whiskey, they got another horse from the Sheriff of Teton County, a splendid sorrel. And then they tried it again with the same result.

Ed Jones' horse came across and the same man that had the trouble before pulled the horse over on him and the horse was drowned. The efforts were abandoned and I was much surprised. I don't believe any of those men ever rode a horse in swimming water before. I commented on this in camp that night and told them how a bad man would cross the stream with bullets whistling around him and they saw the logic of it.

The next day I went to Lander. When I got there I had a call from the Fox people to take a band of fifteen Indians to Philadelphia for a prologue for *The Iron Horse* which was going to open in the Fox Theater there soon. So I gathered up a bunch and went.

Before going I wired Harry Bailey, the Fox man there, to get me a good place to camp my Indians.

He wired back, "I have a splendid place to set your tepees in Fairmount Park and within six blocks of the theater."

I have lots of trouble getting a place to set our tepees as there is no room in these big cities. And I have lots of trouble feeding the Indians when I have to take them to eating houses. I have stopped in a restaurant more than once and asked the proprietor if he could feed 15–25 Indians for me. He would look at them and would have a few stiff collars eating in the place and, shrugging his shoulders, would say, "I don't think I want them."

All I could do was to look farther.

Most people think the Indians are dirty, lousy and thieving and don't want them around. But they are very curious to see them. Hotels, as a rule, do not want them.

E.J. Farlow traveled throughout the United States and Europe with Indians from the Wind River Indian Reservation to present live prologues to the films in which the Indians had appeared. Here Farlow is seen on the stage of the Acme Theatre in Riverton with a group of Indians from the reservation. (Photo courtesy of Pioneer Museum, Lander)

When we arrived in Philadelphia we were met by movie cameras, police, rubbernecks and reporters. These reporters are regular detectives and look things over closely for frauds. And if you are a fraud they do not hesitate to tell the world. When they looked these old warriors over and tried to talk to them and saw them they knew they were looking at real, old, reservation Indians.

Harry Bailey said, "Since wiring you, we found out there was a city ordinance prohibiting camping in the park." So we had to go to a hotel that night and it was still and hot and stuffy in these rooms for the Indians. They never slept a wink and the fire engines went tearing by in the night. They thought the hotel was on fire.

In the morning they said, "Get us out of here."

Bailey and I got a car and hunted for some time and finally got a place on a little stream called Cobb Creek outside the city limits and about eight miles from the theater. We had to hire a big bus to haul the Indians to and from the theater and paid $15 a day for it.

We appeared on the stage four times a day. The theater was splendid and it seated about 2,500 people. We had crowded houses all the time.

When we first arrived one of the stage men, an old-timer in the business, asked me "How long are you booked for?"

I told him two weeks and he said we would do well if we lasted a week as the people there were hard to please. They were used to the best and that this was the graveyard of many troupes and movies. This made me feel very blue but I told him we had a two-week contract and a round-trip ticket in my pocket.

We appeared on the stage four times a day for two weeks and they held us one week more. We had a full house all the time and the last show we appeared in they turned away 5,000, so they said. I never saw a more appreciative audience than we had there. I have appeared on the stage in Chicago, New York, Denver, Hollywood, Boston, London and Paris and several minor places but these were the finest people I had seen.

We were very well treated in Philadelphia and were invited to go out several times. I was invited to talk to the young men and boys at Gerard College and at 9:30 in the morning I was there. A splendid bunch of boys were there and I told them something of the Indians and talked for fifteen minutes and then excused myself. They shouted and clapped and called for more until the president asked me to continue. So I talked to them for fifteen minutes more and told them of the wonders of the Yellowstone National Park. I said that they should see the park if it is possible for them to do so for it is the grandest sight in America and perhaps one of the greatest wonders of the world.

When we had gotten safely fixed in our camp our publicity man said, "There is a place in this town to camp these Indians and I am going to find it." In two or three days he came to me and said, "I have found it."

I asked him where and he replied, "In the treaty made by William Penn with the Indians for the State of Pennsylvania there was a clause that said there is a place to be set aside in the city of Philadelphia for the Indians to set up his tepee when he comes to visit his white brother. It is about thirty feet square, near the Penn Building and surrounded with high walls."

He asked me if I wanted to put a tepee there and I told him, "No, you might as well put an Indian in jail as to camp him in a hole like that."

After we had been showing about a week we received an invitation to take dinner with a Dr. Woodward. We accepted and on the following Sunday Dr. Woodward's car called for me and Harry Bailey. The bus took the Indians and we went to his home. It was a magnificent mansion on a hill, commanding a splendid view. It was up the Schuylkill River, I believe. After arriving there we were looking over the grounds and Miss Woodward, a splendid girl (or woman I might call her), asked the Indians to stand by a fountain so that she might take a picture of them.

I had them arranged to suit her and after taking the picture she said, "We were in the Jackson Hole in Wyoming three weeks ago today."

"Is that so," I replied. "I was there myself."

"Yes, I saw you there and that is why we asked you here today. I saw you on the stage and recognized you."

I asked if she saw them drown the horse.

"Yes," she replied, "and I heard what you said about it."

"What did I say?" I asked.

She replied that it would not look well in print—something about damn fools.

We had a splendid feast about five o'clock in the evening and they set a splendid table for the Indians. They like to have bursted eating and when they were through the table was still loaded with good things to eat. Some of the Indian women took some of the fruit and put it in a bandanna and took it with them.

When they were through the Indians asked to see their host and hostess. I asked the Woodwards in as they were in the next room. Old Goes-in-the-Lodge rose up and thanked them for this good food and said they were the best friends the Indians had found in Philadelphia. He said that the Indians would always remember them as their good friends. This was all said in Arapaho and was interpreted to them.

I apologized to Mrs. Woodward for the Indians carrying off some of the victuals from the table and told her that an Indian thinks that when you set food in front of him it is for him to take all he wants of it. She was glad they did this and seemed pleased with the satisfied manner of the Indians. I will say that the Woodwards were some of the nicest people I have ever met and we all went away from Philadelphia with a very warm spot in our hearts for the good people there.

TRIP TO BOSTON

ROM PHILADELPHIA WE went to Boston and appeared on the stage with *The Iron Horse* at the Tremont Temple Theater for two weeks. We had a very good time in Boston.

We were invited out several times and one of these times was to the Children's Hospital. I was greatly impressed with these little ones. There must have been a hundred or more of these sick and crippled little ones and their little faces looked so pitiful. Some of them seemed frightened at the big Indians but I told them they would not hurt any of them and that they would do anything in the world to help them if they could. We had a very pleasant hour and some of the little ones asked many questions about them, all of which I was glad to answer. I do not remember the name of this hospital but the nurses were a grand lot of good women and they enjoyed seeing the little ones look at the Indians.

We were in Boston about a week when we received an invitation to call on the governor and we gladly accepted. At about eleven o'clock A.M. we called at the state house and were ushered into the presence of the governor, Alvan T. Fuller. We spent a pleasant half-hour with him and some of his staff.

The Indians put on a few steps of the Wolf Dance for their amusement and we were about ready to go when I said to the governor, "These people will give you a name by which you will be known to them and if you like I will have them give it to you now."

He replied that it would please him very much for them to do so. So the Indians got together and selected a name for the governor and when they had decided upon it I had them come to the center of the room. The governor stood up before them and Goes-in-the-Lodge stepped up to him. Placing a war bonnet on his head, Goes-in-the-Lodge said in Arapaho, "I name you Chief Rising Sun, as you are a friend we have found away in the far east where the sun comes up."

Grasping the governor's hand he continued, "I now accept you as a brother and friend of the Arapahos."

Raising his hands heavenward Goes-in-the-Lodge said, "May the Great Spirit of the white man make sunshine in your heart and may your heart be ever kind to the Indian. May you always be the friend of the Indian for the Indian needs the white man for this friend and not his enemy. For this we thank you, Great Spirit."

This was ended with "Na Hoe, Na Hoe," which means "Thank you, thank you, thank you."

I interpreted all of this to the governor when Goes-in-the-Lodge ceased speaking. To make the governor a brother was the highest honor they could bestow on him. The governor is now an Arapaho Indian and his name is Chief Rising Sun and he is eligible to sit in the councils of his tribe.

The war bonnet that we used belonged to one of the Indians and we had to have it for the stage, otherwise we would have given it to him. I told him I would get him one as soon as I could but it was more than a year before I could get a suitable one. The eagle feathers were getting very scarce and a good war bonnet is made out of six feathers out of the tail of the eagle. There are twelve feathers in the tail but only six are considered first class. The bonnet I sent to the governor contained ninety feathers. This bonnet was made by Black Horse and his wife and it took them some time to get the feathers and material to make it. After it was made a council was called and I attended it. I told them the bonnet was for Chief Rising Sun and that I was going to write him a letter and send it to him. The council very solemnly had the medicine man bless the bonnet and all those present and it was sent with the best wishes of his red brothers and the wish that his enemies would fall before him.

We appeared on the stage in Boston for two weeks and then took the train for home. The Indians are always glad to get home and they always make a feast fund when they are out. Everyone gives some money out of their wages and I am always called upon to donate pretty heavily. Any money they get for outside work on these trips goes in the feast fund. When they get home and the weather is favorable they put on a feast for all their friends and neighbors. That means the entire tribe, or as many of them as cares to come. They buy beef, bread, coffee, sugar and prunes and have a great feast. If the food is sufficient it sometimes lasts two or three days and there is dancing at night and they have a good time. The Indians at home look forward to this homecoming and to this feast very eagerly and would be very much disappointed if no fund had been established. I am generally made the custodian of these funds.

One of their favorite ways to feed this fund is with their games. They gamble quite a little when out and when an Indian wins a pot that is of much importance it is tolled for the feast fund. Sometimes they have handed me quite a sum after one of their games. They are great for playing Monte with cards and are very shrewd at it according to several white men who have tried to beat them. The bunch I had in Philadelphia learned to play poker and played it most of the time on this trip. But they bet very sparingly. A fifty-cent bet is a big one for them.

MAKING WAR PAINT

I N AUGUST OF 1926 I received word from the MGM studio at Culver City, California to meet their manager, Mr. Bishoff, Colonel McCoy and their director, Van Dyke, at Rock Springs and take them to Lander and the Wind River Reservation. We were to look up a location for the making of a big Indian picture called *War Paint*.

After two days of scouting around the location was selected. It was in the mouth of the Little Wind River Canyon. I was asked to furnish 150 wild Indians with feathers, beads and paint. This picture was made around the scene of a famous battle between the Crow Indians and Shoshone Indians in about 1862.

As near as I can get it, the Shoshones were camped just below the mouth of this canyon when a band of Crow warriors made a raid and attempted to get away with the Shoshone's horses. But the Shoshones were too quick for them and cut off a large part of their horses and chased about twenty of the Crow Indians up the canyon. The Crows retreated far up the canyon and at last took refuge in a large cave in the rocks and barricaded themselves. It was impossible for the Shoshones to get them.

The Shoshones got above the mouth of this cave and rolled timber, brush and firewood down in front of it and then set it afire to suffocate the Crows.

This cave had a second cave behind it but it was difficult for a man to squeeze his body through the small passage connecting the two. All but four of the Crows had crawled through this passage. The other four were found dead in the outer cave. The inner cave has since been visited by but three persons that I know of and the skeletons of seventeen Crow warriors still lay in this inner cave. There was not a man or boy in the making of this picture who had the nerve to crawl through this narrow passage far down in the ground to see the sight that lay beyond. But most of the people in the picture went and viewed the outer cave.

This picture, starring Colonel Tim McCoy and Pauline Stark, had for a scene one of the finest Indian villages of over fifty Indian tepees that I have seen since the old days of the Indian. Most of the Indians are living in houses or tents now and the tepee is getting to be a lost art. The old Sweat Lodges, Dog Tepees, Travois and Medicine Lodges are also a thing of the past and are seldom seen in any Indian village.

In the making of this picture we used many Indians for the first time and they took a great interest in it. It is needless to say that the Indians take keen delight in the making of these pictures and get a great kick out of them.

In one of the scenes Colonel McCoy was to be captured and pulled from his horse by the Indians. They were waiting just around the corner of a building and he had ridden over them twice but they had failed to get him. I told them they must be sure and get him this time and they were to close in on him from both sides.

The Colonel's horse was very high spirited and hard to catch. He would shy and strike at the Indians and they were afraid of him. He came on for the third time and I said, "Now get him." They sprang at the horse but failed. As he rode past an old Shoshone with a big gun loaded with a blank cartridge and blank powder pulled down on the Colonel. At a distance of about ten feet he shot him off his horse. The force of the powder hit Colonel McCoy in the point of the right shoulder, neck and head, and knocked him off his horse.

There was great confusion as it was thought at first he was killed. But he was badly burned by the powder.

When I scolded the Indian for the shooting Colonel Mc-Coy, he soberly said "You said to get him and I got him."

In one of the battle scenes where the Shoshones were having a hand-to-hand fight, the director suddenly stopped and said, "Farlow, get those Indians to look serious, they are fighting each other and laughing." It seemed very funny to them and I had quite a time to get a fighting expression on them.

That play fight was the biggest joke they had seen for a long time. Those rubber knives, swords, and pistols were a joke to them and one of the biggest jokes they had was when one of the Indians got one of the rubber knives. It was the first rubber knife he had ever seen. Baring his breast to the sun and the Great Spirit he bid his friends good-bye and said he was going to the happy hunting grounds. With a long, swinging stroke of his arm he pretended to drive the knife to his heart and dropped to the ground pretending to be dead. His friends very solemnly began to cry and mourn and make a big fuss over him. A lot of the Indians and whites thought he really was dead. His friends rolled him in a blanket and took him to a crevice in the rocks where they were going to bury him. They began to put rocks on him when he suddenly came alive. But they told him he was dead and insisted on burying him. He was scared stiff before they finally let him go.

TRIP TO HOLLYWOOD

I N NOVEMBER OF 1926 I was called upon to take a band of twenty Indians to Hollywood for the MGM Corporation. We worked in Griffith Park and at the MGM ranch at the north end of Laurel Canyon for two weeks in the making of a picture called *The Winning of the Wilderness* which starred Colonel McCoy and Joan Crawford. For this picture we shipped thirty tepees to California and left them there as the property of MGM.

In this picture we burned a man at the stake and it was hard for the Indians to refrain from burning him a little as many of them wanted to do. Nothing out of the ordinary occurred in the making of this picture but we were invited out one night to a very fine residence and had a dandy feed. The hostess—I will not give her name—was overcome with the presence of so many real old blanket Indians and she danced and tried to sing Indian. She finally fell in a swoon on the floor. A doctor had to be called and the Indians got out of there, as the saying is, right now.

One Indian—Two Strikes—was hit in the breast by her with all her might and he fled. The banquet was but half over and they wanted the Indians to go back and finish. But no, they said. "White woman crazy, bad medicine." And they still talk about the crazy white woman in California.

In August of 1927 the same company came back to the Wind River Reservation and called upon me for 150 Indians again. This time the manager was Art Smith. Colonel McCoy and Dorothy Sebastian were to star in a picture called *Wyoming*.

We worked in much the same territory and with the same Indians as we did before. In this picture much of the work was done around the old block house near the old agency. The building was built sixty years ago by four trappers and squatters. It was made of stone with a dirt roof and loop holes, and a well was dug inside. Provisions were stored inside so the occupants could exist for a month or so if necessary. The old building still stands and the grave of Sacajawea is about a mile from there as is the grave of Chief Washakie.

The United States Indian Agent Paul Haas, while willing to let the Indians take part in these movies, says it is demoralizing to the Indians and they lose interest in their agricultural pursuits. He also says these movies revive old legends, customs, songs, dances and traditions and it is some time before they get settled down again.

The Indian, when I first knew him, was far different than he is today. Then they were proud, haughty and independent; kings in their own domain with an empire for their hunting grounds. And until the white man said stop, they knew no ruler. The Indian, as a race, never knew what it was to be despised. Far from aspiring to be like the white man, he has looked forward with a feeling of dread to the coming of the day when he would lose his ethnic individuality.

LOOKING BACK AT THE AMERICAN INDIAN

A FEW YEARS AGO I was talking to a splendid audience of about 600 people at the Old Faithful Inn at the upper geyser basin in Yellowstone Park. I had drawn a word picture of the American Indian being driven from the Atlantic into the Pacific Ocean by the advancing power of the white man and had just stated that one of the saddest and most impressive pictures I had ever seen was of the Indian standing on a cliff overlooking the Pacific Ocean, his broken spear and unstrung bow lying at his feet, gazing out at the setting of the sun, of his destiny going down in the west.

A gentleman in the audience, a minister of the gospel from Denver, spoke up and said, "Mr. Farlow, don't you think it is better that the white man has taken this country from the Indians? I can see clearly the hand of God in the setting aside of the American Indian and the establishing thereon a higher and better religion and civilization."

I said, "Friend, that is a pretty big question for me to answer. I do not know whether I can answer it or not, but will say this. If you look at it from a commercial standpoint there is no doubt but that the white man has made greater and more intensive use of this country than the Indian would perhaps in a thousand years. But if you look at it from the standpoint of right and justice and honesty and fair dealing, it takes on an entirely different appearance. Suppose there came from the west a race of people as much more numerous and powerful as we were over the

American Indian and they swept us back into the Atlantic Ocean, setting our remnants aside on reservations here and there and establishing on the continent a higher and better civilization and religion—from their point of view. Do you still see the hand of God as clearly as you did before?

"That is an exact comparison of the situation.

"I am often asked if these Indians are civilized and I say, 'If you mean are they learned in letters, arts and sciences, I will say no. If you mean are they educated in all the wiles and arts of lying, stealing, cheating, skulduggery and deception that the white man is adept in, I will say no. But if you mean from the standpoint of the Golden Rule, I will say that he ranks well up with the white race.'

"I want to impress this truth upon you. The Indian has been sadly misrepresented to the younger generation of novelists, story writers and even historians. He has been represented as cruel, crafty, treacherous, blood-thirsty and degraded. But in my brief experience of fifty years of almost constant contact and communication with most of the leading tribes of the west, I have not that opinion.

"The Indian hates the white man with a just hate and he has tried for the last 100 years to stop the white man. But to no avail. I have sat in the tepees of many of the older Indians in the early days of my acquaintance with them and heard them tell of their adventures and experiences and their struggles. They struggled to retain certain pieces of hunting grounds only to lose them in the end. Then they fell back and tried to hold another place with the same result. The story of the Indian always has the same ending—always to lose.

"It is sweet to taste the fruits of victory but the American Indian has drank long and deep of the bitter dregs of humiliation and despair and disappointment and defeat."

ADOPTED INTO THE
ARAPAHO TRIBE

THERE WAS A COUNCIL meeting held at Fort Washakie in the month of April, 1931. At this council meeting there was present the entire Shoshone Council of seven, the entire Arapaho Council of seven, and the agent, Paul Haas. At this council the agent was told to either ask for a transfer or resign.

My name was mentioned at this meeting and immediately the agent spoke up and said, "Ed Farlow is not an Indian and has no business on this reservation and I do not want him interfering with our affairs."

Some of the older Arapahos at once came to me and said, "Are you not an Arapaho?"

I said, "No, not officially. I was a made a member of your tribe at a dance more than fifty years ago and have been recognized as an Arapaho by the tribe. But the government has no record of it and does not recognize me."

They at once said, "We will make you a member now if you are willing."

I said, "Go ahead."

Notice was at once sent to all the Indians to gather at the old dance hall of the Arapahos. And on the 21st of June, 1931 there gathered almost the entire tribe. Mr. L.L. Newton, editor of the *Wyoming State Journal*, was present and had this to say of the gathering.

In his later years, E.J. Farlow posed with part of his family, including his son Jule, grandson Jule, and great-grandson Edward Jule Farlow III. The group includes (back row, left to right) R.G. Gallinger (son-in-law to Jule Farlow), Jule Farlow, Jr. Jule Farlow, Etta Farlow (second wife of Jule Farlow), Iona Gallinger (daughter of Jule Farlow); (front row) Diane Gallinger (daughter of R.G. and Iona Gallinger), Victoria Rae Farlow (daughter of Jule Farlow, Jr.), Edward Jule Farlow III (son of Jule Farlow, Jr.) E.J. Farlow, and Robert W. Gallinger (son of R.G. and Iona Gallinger). (Photo courtesy of Pioneer Museum, Lander.)

"Ed J. Farlow, for fifty years a counselor and friend of the Arapahos, lost two names and received a new one from his Indian friends Friday night in a solemn and impressive ceremony in which he was formally made a member of the tribe and will now be know by them as Ne a he Bah a, meaning Red Eagle.

"Red Eagle was a noted warrior and leader of the tribe before the time of Black Coal and Sharp Nose. His memory has been carried down to the present tribesmen in tradition and story for he was brave and wise, always kind but fearless and exemplified in his life all the ideals of Indian manhood. Farlow has been known as Nish ki ah, the Whip, meaning a fast worker, a driver, a giver of inspiration, a leader, a man who gets things done and done quickly. Others have called him Naw te Neh Baa e, Sioux old man.

"The scene was at the dance hall of the lower Arapahos near St. Stephen's Mission. Three hundred or more Indians were seated on the grass in a circle. The feast was in the center. It was a gift from Mr. Farlow who had brought a young beef, two fat sheep, 100 loaves of bread, twenty-five pounds of coffee and fifty of sugar. Coffee had been cooked, the meat prepared and it waited for two hours and more for the ceremonies and dances to conclude before being served.

"Painted Wolf, Sam Wolfrang, chief of the tribe, was dressed in gala attire. His beautiful eagle feather head dress, tunic of bright flowered design, beaded leggings and bright blanket made up his adornment. On either side sat the head men of the tribe, two in dance ceremony dress.

"The drummers and singers were seated on the ground just inside the circle. A few resonant beats of the drum and the singers swung into the high pitches of the dance songs. George White Antelope was the announcer. He spoke in Arapaho and all was quiet save the crying of babies and the barking of dogs at times. Order and reverence marked the occasion for it was a ceremony which meant much to the Indians.

"Chief Painted Wolf made the opening speech. He told of the friendship the Indians had for the brother they were about to make a member of the tribe and give a new name. He has been true to them, he said, always helped them in their troubles and advised them in their problems. They wanted someone with wisdom and authority to represent them in matters of pressing importance and gave this good reason for making this man a member of the tribe in fact although he had been so regarded for many years. Mr. Farlow was called to his feet and with face to the center and folded arms, stood erect while Chief Painted Wolf directly behind placed his left hand on his back. His speech was short and ended in a prayer to the Great Spirit. Every hat and head dress was taken off as the chief removed his and slipped his blanket down from his shoulders for this invocation. Educated Indians said the prayer was a beautiful one and implored the Deity to watch over the Indians, to heal their sick and comfort those whose homes had been saddened by death. The souls of the departed were blessed by commending them to the One whom the redskin worships.

"Standing beside the candidate the Chief threw one of Farlow's names to the ground. It was Sioux Old Man, and a mature woman with hastening steps came across the circle, rubbed her hands in the grass and "picked it up." She will henceforth be known as Sioux Old Man.

"Thinking the ceremony completed, Farlow turned when he was faced by a younger mother, Bridget Washington, with babe in arms. She asked for his old name. When Farlow in sign language told her she was too late. It was the second name, The Whip, she wanted for her boy and it was given.

"Congratulations and handshaking followed and the ceremonies of initiation were over. Farlow was now a member of the tribe.

"For the Indians the night was young and there was more to be done. The announcer spoke again and like sinners in the old-time revival meetings, coming to the altar, Indian woman formed a segment within the circle. The singers and drums gave the Chief dance, and medicine men with red paint anointed the foreheads and cheeks of those who came. These women were in mourning. They had lost some member of the family and the ceremony of painting marked the time that they would no longer mourn but would be happy and forget their sorrow. The Crow dance concluded this ceremony.

"Again the announcer spoke. This time he would have a speech from their new brother and Mr. Farlow, with an interpreter, stood again within the circle. Mr. Farlow said a few sentences and then the interpreter translated it into the Arapaho language. He said that he was highly honored by being made a member of the Arapaho tribe, that he had been among them for fifty years and was here before they came, that he had enjoyed his association with them, had done what he could to help the Indians and would continue in the future as he had in the past to be a help to the Arapahos, his brothers.

"The Wolf dance and song brought out more dancers while the committee prepared to distribute the feast. The bread was cut in third loaf chunks, the meat in generous handsful and the coffee poured into the cups. There was food for all and it was a happy satisfied crowd of Indians which scattered to their tents and tepees at near midnight."

CONCLUSION

Now the last fifty years I have said "How" to the American Indian almost as often as I have saluted those of my own kind. And if from my long contact and experience with the red man of the west I have come to know him intimately and understandingly, I have earned the right to speak of him as I know him.

I believe I know the Indian and believe the Indian was a man before outrage and oppression made of him a savage. I have known him as a savage and as a fighting man in the pride and insolence of his strength. I have known him as a monarch whipped into submission. I have known him as a sage in council. And I have known him as a beggar with the pride starved out of him.

I have smoked with him the pipe of peace and I have sat with him at his feasts and in his councils. And when I compare them all—the red and the white race—calmly in my own mind, their vices and virtues, their sterling worth and their shortcomings, the Indian does not suffer by comparison.

When you see an Indian sitting on the curb or standing on the corner with that faraway expression upon his countenance, indifferent to the fate or progress of the world, remember that the white man has taken his country and made him what he is today—a nation conquered and a people dispossessed. His pride is humbled, and his spirit is subdued. His heart is broken. As a race his sun is set.

INDEX

ABOUT THE AUTHOR

THE WEST AND ED FARLOW grew up together. Farlow was just sixteen years old in 1876 when, after hearing exciting tales of western adventures, he and a friend hopped a freight train for Laramie, Wyoming. The young Wyoming Territory was only eight years old itself, and it would be twelve years before Wyoming achieved statehood.

Farlow was in Wyoming before the Battle of Little Big Horn and the tragedy at the White River Agency run by Nathaniel Meeker. He was on the range before the Winter of 1986–87 that signaled the end of the open-range cattle era and foreshadowed the Johnson County War. He had located in the Lander area by 1878 and knew the woman known on the Wind River Reservation as Sacajawea. It has been said that Ed Farlow was there when the West was born.

Wind Rivers Adventures is the first publication of the memoirs of Edward J. Farlow. He wrote these accounts in the late 1930s and early 1940s when he was between seventy-five and eighty-five years old. He lived to be ninety and was active and vigorous until near the end of his life. And what a life it was!

His obituary in the *Wyoming State Journal* reported that he always had a place of honor in the Lander Pioneer Days parade and was considerably peeved in 1950 when at the age of eighty-nine he was consigned to an automobile rather than being allowed to ride his favorite saddlehorse in the parade.

247

The accounts in this book record much of the life of Edward J. Farlow. However, these stories end in 1931 while Farlow himself lived another twenty years.

He was born near Adel, Iowa, on January 2, 1861. He arrived in Laramie in April 1876 and worked as a cowboy, first near Laramie and later near the gold fields in the South Pass country.

In 1880, he returned to Iowa and convinced his brother Nelson to travel back with him to the Lander, Wyoming, area which he had come to love while working near South Pass. The trip with a team and wagon took them forty days. Brothers Henry and Elbert (Zeke) joined them in Wyoming before long.

In the fall of 1880, Ed, Nelson, and Zeke became equal partners in purchasing one hundred head of yearling heifers for eleven dollars each. Farlow counted out the eleven hundred dollars to W.P. Noble onto a saddle blanket and thus became a cattleman. Ed looked after the brothers' cattle but he kept his paying job, working as a cowboy for R. H. Hall.

In the fall of 1881, he gathered the Farlow market cattle together with those from four other outfits and trailed 1250 head to the railroad near Rawlins, Wyoming, for shipping. Years later he reported to a local newspaper that he trailed a herd of beef to the railroad near either Casper or Rawlins every year from 1881 to 1905, missing only three years.

The winter of 1882–83 was a bad one and the Farlow brothers suffered heavy losses as did most other area stockmen. Ed hired out to Jules Lamoreaux, a stockman of French-Canadian ancestry with substantial holdings.

In 1883, when Farlow was twenty-two, he married Elizabeth (Lizzie) Lamoreaux, the daughter of Jules and Elizabeth (Woman Dress) Lamoreaux. Woman Dress was the sister of Chief Gall, who led the Sioux in the Battle of Little Big Horn. The Lamoreaux's daughter Lizzie was born in 1864 at Fort Laramie and was educated at a Catholic convent in Quebec. She was considered the belle of Lander and had won the title of "most popular girl" at the Catholic Church bazaar.

Ed and Lizzie were the parents of two sons: Jule and Albert (Stub). Stub later achieved fame as a rodeo cowboy and is believed by some to be the model for the cowboy silhouetted atop a bucking horse which is the symbol of Wyoming. Ed and Lizzie also raised May Cantley from childhood after she was orphaned.

Farlow's obituary in the *Wyoming State Journal* said, "Their home was one of open-hearted hospitality. On their lawn an Indian lodge stood, a well equipped tepee for the friends of the Indian race, they gave liberally to the Wyoming Children's Home Finding Society and Mrs. Farlow was active with the group of women who furnished garments and other supplies to that institution."

Soon after Farlow married Lizzie, he was in charge of the "L" outfit belonging to Jules Lamoreaux, consisting of about five thousand head of cattle.

In 1894, Farlow held what is believed to be the first paid admission rodeo in the world on his place on the outskirts of Lander. The annual celebration grew until it became the Lander Pioneer Days, still celebrated today. For twenty-five years Farlow owned the grounds where the rodeo was held and, during that time, he directed many of the shows. He has been recognized as the inventor of the relay race and for his construction of the race track, grandstand and stables which hosted what was then called "Frontier Days."

Farlow and the Fremont County community were convinced that the name Frontier Days was stolen by the Cheyenne celebration. The *Wyoming State Journal* reported in the October 23, 1936, issue that, "In 1908 Charles Irwin came to Lander to one of the shows and went back to Cheyenne and told them he had learned how to put on a wild west show. They stole the name, 'Frontier Days' from Lander and had it copyrighted, and from then their show began to grow."

Farlow reports that same sequence in this book. Actually, however, the Cheyenne event was called Frontier Days before the turn of the century. But, it is quite possible that Charles Irwin honed his own considerable showmanship skills by watching Ed Farlow in action in Lander.

About this time Farlow was also involved with his father-in-law in a meat retailing business in Lander.

Soon Farlow was able to acquire his own piece of land near Lander. The *Journal* obituary reported, "Using his squatter's right in 1897 he settled on the lower Northfork of the Popo Agie on the Wind River Indian Reservation, which land was later allotted to Mrs. Farlow due to her Sioux Indian heritage."

⚒

Beginning in 1907, Farlow became interested in the sheep business. He was one of the first in the area to build extensive lambing sheds for more successful early spring lambing. In 1910, he was appointed as a member of the State Board of Sheep Commissioners, a position he held under four governors, often serving as the chairman.

Shortly after arriving in the Lander Valley, Farlow had learned the languages of the Arapaho and the Shoshone and acquired the ability to use sign language. This ability to communicate in tribal languages, the location of his ranch on the reservation, his wife's Indian ancestry, plus his genuine affection for the Indians allowed Farlow to gain their friendship and confidence. He maintained a long friendship with Chief Washakie.

In 1913, he traveled with a group of thirty-five Arapaho to Denver as guests of the national conclave of the Knights Templar. The Indians set up eight tepees and entertained the crowds.

Over 40,000 people gathered and the police had to be called to maintain order.

The next year, Farlow accompanied about seventy-five Indians and twenty-five cowboys and cowgirls to Casper for a three-day celebration. In 1916, he traveled with twenty-five Indians to Fort Collins. For several years, he regularly accompanied Indian groups to shows in Rawlins, Riverton, and Lander as well as being involved in arranging celebrations on the reservation.

In 1922, upon the recommendation of Colonel Tim McCoy, Farlow was selected to organize the appearance of the Indians in the big budget silent movie *The Covered Wagon*. Filmed in Utah and directed by James Cruze, the motion picture is now considered the prototype for the western genre. It was an instant hit. Perhaps as many as one hundred Indians appeared in the film.

At the time, a popular way to promote movies was to precede the showing with a live performance. Farlow and a smaller group of Indians worked for three months in Hollywood performing a prologue of exhibitions.

The Indian prologue was such a hit that the film company decided to open the film in London with the same prologue. So Ed Farlow and a group of Wind River Reservation Indians traveled to Chicago, New York, London and Paris.

Farlow eventually accompanied groups of Indians on twenty-seven trips from coast to coast and to Europe. They appeared in the movies *The Thundering Herd*, *The Iron Horse*, *War Paint*, *The Winning of the Wilderness*, *Wyoming*, and *Three Bad Men* produced by major Hollywood studios such as MGM, Fox, and Famous Players Lasky. The movies starred luminaries such as Joan Crawford, Colonel Tim McCoy, and Pauline Stark. Some of the movies were introduced by live prologues which involved additional travel to Philadelphia, Boston, and other cities.

Farlow was proud that the Indians in his charge were treated with respect and returned home healthy. Additionally, he was able to negotiate quite respectable wages for the groups.

During the time he was traveling to performances he was also active in the community. He was the mayor of Lander from 1923-27, and he was a member of the school board.

But perhaps the most unique thing about Ed Farlow was his appreciation of the Indians and Indian culture. The *Wyoming State Journal* wrote, "[Farlow] helped the Indians more than any other white man in Fremont County. When the railroad was built into Lander he solicited the Division Superintendent...to employ the Indians on the track work and right-of- way.... He had them learn to shear sheep on his own flocks and solicited other sheepmen to employ them...and he has fed more Indians at his camps, his ranch and at his home than any other white man in Fremont county. No Indian ever went away from Ed Farlow's camps or ranch or home hungry. He openly protested the sale of the Tribal herd a few years ago, which deprived the Indians of one of the finest herds of white-faced cattle in the State. He is strong for the restocking of the reservation with cattle...and is doing all in his power to reach the 'higher ups' to get the Maverick Springs oil field into production as the royalty from these wells would be a great help to the Indians."

In 1931, Farlow's position on the reservation was questioned as he was a white man living on the Indian land. As a result, on June 21, 1931, he was formally made a member of the Arapaho Tribe. In a ceremony involving almost every tribal member, he was given the name Red Eagle which replaced the two names by which he had previously been known among the tribes: the Whip and Sioux Old Man. It was one of Farlow's proudest moments.

In the summer of 1932, Lizzie Farlow died. She and Ed had been married for forty-nine years.

Ed and Lizzie had been active in the Lander Pioneers group which he had helped start in 1886. They had helped supervise the erection of the Pioneer Cabin which housed many relics of pioneer days. Among Ed and Lizzie's friends in the Lander Pioneers was Mrs. Cora Crowley, a widow with grown children. Mrs. Crowley was involved in the improvement of the Pioneer Cabin and especially in the beautification of the grounds with flowers and landscaping. In October 1933, Ed Farlow and Mrs. Cora Crowley were married at Pioneer Cabin.

Ed was elected to the Wyoming State Legislature in 1932 and 1934. He was defeated in 1936 by a close margin. He served terms as Justice of the Police and Police Judge and was a stockholder and vice-president of the Stockgrowers Bank.

In December 1944, Cora Crowley Farlow passed away. After her passing, Farlow made his home with his son Jule. In 1949 at age eighty-eight, Farlow sold his ranch on the Wind River Reservation.

Farlow was known as a great showman and a popular storyteller. The *Wyoming State Journal* article announcing his marriage to Cora Crowley says, "It was a memorable group of pioneer people, each who had a part in the building of this west and many reminiscences were told with the genial Ed keeping the company in laughter in recounting the high spots of Lander life during the past half century."

In his last days, Farlow made a trip to retrace his route from Adel, Iowa, to Wyoming. This time he traveled by private plane. The trip that had taken his brother Nelson and him forty days with a team and wagon, this time took only four-and-one-half hours. It was a measurable demonstration of how much the country had changed during his lifetime.

Ed Farlow died on April 8, 1951, at 7 A.M. in Bishop Randall hospital in Lander. His funeral was held on April 11 at the

Methodist Church; he was buried at the Mount Hope Cemetery. He was ninety years old. In photographs he seems to have
become even more handsome and dignified-looking as he aged.
He had a full head of white wavy hair and a bushy moustache
into his ninetieth year.

Edward J. Farlow had been there when Wyoming was born.
He and the West spread their wings together.

The text is composed in
twelve point Adobe Garamond.
Display type is Trajan;
decorative type is SMC Border Dingbats 1
The book is printed on
sixty-pound Joy White Offset
acid-free paper
by Thomson-Shore.